THE TWO SAINTS WAY

A pilgrimage route between the
cathedral cities of Chester and Lichfield

David Pott

Northern Eye

Northern Eye Books

Published in 2019 by
Northern Eye Books,
Tattenhall,
Cheshire, CH3 9PX

www.northerneyebooks.co.uk

ISBN 978-1-908632-92-0

Copyright © David Pott 2019

David Pott has asserted his right under the Copyright, Designs and Patents Act, 1988 to be identified as the author of this work.

All rights reserved.

A CIP catalogue record for this book is available from the British Library.

Whilst every effort has been made to ensure that the information in this book is correct at the time of publication, neither the author nor the publisher can accept any responsibility for any errors, loss or injury, however caused.

The routes described in this book are undertaken at the individual's own risk. The publisher and copyright owners accept no responsibility for any consequences arising from the use of this book, including misinterpretation of the maps and directions.

This book contains mapping data licensed from the Ordnance Survey with the permission of the Controller of Her Majesty's Stationery Office.

© Crown copyright 2019. All rights reserved. Licence number 100047867

CONTENTS

Introduction	4
Planning your Journey	6
Accommodation	7
Two Saints Way Stages	8
Waymarking and Signage	11
Visiting Sites	12
Additional Advice and the Countryside Code	12
The Story of the Two Saints Way	13
Who were the Two Saints?	15
Connecting Medieval and Contemporary Pilgrimage	20
The Cathedral Cities	22

The Way of St Chad (Chester to Lichfield)

Section 1	Chester to Nantwich	30
Section 2	Nantwich to Stoke	44
Section 3	Stoke to Stafford	66
Section 4	Stafford to Lichfield	92

The Way of St Werburgh (Lichfield to Chester)

Section 4	Lichfield to Stafford	112
Section 3	Stafford to Stoke	120
Section 2	Stoke to Nantwich	128
Section 1	Nantwich to Chester	138

Introduction

The Two Saints Way is a 92 mile (148 km) long-distance walking route between the cathedral cities of Chester and Lichfield. It has been set up in such a way as to recover some of the aspects that were important in medieval pilgrimage and to apply them to a contemporary context.

You can walk the route in either direction.

If you journey from Chester to Lichfield the easier part is at the beginning and this gives you time to prepare for the rather hillier sections in Staffordshire. If you walk from Lichfield to Chester, the best time of year is between October and March when the sun is behind you in the south. This yields much better views.

The route is divided into four sections:

SECTION 1
Chester to Nantwich - 23.5 miles

Starting at Chester Cathedral and passing by the pilgrim church of St John, the route is mostly along the Shropshire Union Canal, with diversions to Christleton, the dramatic Beeston Castle, the pleasant village of Bunbury, a short stretch of the Llangollen Canal and historic St Mary's Acton before ending at the fine market town of Nantwich.

SECTION 2
Nantwich to Stoke-on-Trent - 25.5 miles

Farmland predominates in this second section and after the relative flatness of Cheshire there are some hills to walk over on the way into Stoke-on-Trent, which is notable for its industrial heritage sites and The Potteries Museum where you can see the Staffordshire Anglo-Saxon Hoard.

SECTION 3
Stoke-on-Trent to Stafford - 23 miles

The route follows the Trent Valley along sections of the Trent and Mersey Canal and remnants of the Staffordshire New Forest at Trentham and Tittensor Chase, passing through Stone to Salt where it turns south-west over Hopton Heath and Beacon Hill to the county town of Stafford.

SECTION 4
Stafford to Lichfield - 20 miles

After meandering out of Stafford along the River Sow, the route joins the Heart of England Way to cross Cannock Chase, an Area of Outstanding Natural Beauty, before the last few miles of farmland and country lanes to Lichfield and the pilgrim sites at the Cathedral and St Chad's Well.

Each of these sections has its own chapter with maps and directions to guide you on your way. There are also four stages in each section, making 16 stages in all, of between 3 and 8 miles long. They are designed to coincide with places where public transport is available.

There is also information about interesting places along the route (in separate shaded areas), as well as photographs. Information about Chester and Lichfield are in a separate section on the cathedral cities.

Planning your Journey

Serious long-distance walkers will be able to walk the four sections in four days. However, if you wish to take a more leisurely approach, you can work out alternative plans depending on how much walking you want to do each day and how much time you wish to allocate to visiting the interesting sites along the route. Use the sections on accommodation and transport to plan your journey.

Here is a suggested plan for those who hope to complete the walk in one week. It allows for half a day in both Chester and Lichfield – not only because they are both such interesting cities with a great deal to offer, but also because, in the traditions of pilgrimage, it is good to allow time to prepare yourself at the start and to give time for reflection at the journey's end. This plan can simply be reversed if you choose to walk from Lichfield to Chester.

Day 1	Time for visiting sites and preparation in Chester. Walk to Waverton 5 miles
Day 2	Waverton to Nantwich 18 miles
Day 3	Nantwich to Audley 15 miles
Day 4	Audley to Trentham 17 miles
Day 5	Trentham to Stafford 17 miles
Day 6	Stafford to Cannock Wood 14 miles
Day 7	Cannock Wood to Lichfield with time for visits and ending well. 6 miles

If you prefer generally shorter distances or wish to do the walk over a series of weekends using public transport, you will probably prefer to use the stages system and chart on **page 8-9** to plan your journey and work out transport links. Currently, the part of the journey with the most difficult public transport amenities is the area around Beeston and Bunbury. Please note that all information on buses, timetables and connections should be checked with the relevant bus company as they are liable to seasonal, weekend and term-time variations. This can be done online by searching the company name online. When planning a journey the following websites are very helpful:

www.transportdirect.info
www.travelinemidlands.co.uk
www.traveline-northwest.co.uk

Baggage transfer

A baggage transfer service is available through the organisation: Staffordshire on Foot. Please contact Collin on **collin@cnfc.info** or telephone **07966 132 138** or **01785 823 474** for further information.

Accommodation

We recommend pre-booking your accommodation.
You can find some accommodation options on the website at
twosaintsway.org.uk/?pade_id=401.
There are number of websites that can help you find B&B's including:

www.bedandbreakfastnationwide.com

www.visitus.co.uk

The following information websites give details of accommodation and only give options that have been inspected by Quality in Tourism (VisitEngland), the AA, or properties participating in the Staffordshire Approved Visitor Accommodation Scheme.

www.visitcheshire.com

www.enjoystaffordshire.com

www.visitstoke.co.uk

For campsites see www.ukcampsite.co.uk

Maps

There are maps of all the stages at the start of each of the four sections. Larger maps are also included in the text to give extra information such as street names.

The relevant OS maps for the Two Saints Way are as follows: Landranger 117, 118, 127, 128 and Explorer 266, 257, 258, 244.

A gpx file of the route can be dowloaded from www.twosaintsway.co.uk.

Two Saints Way Stages

NB Transport links are for the second location in column 2.
BR stands for British Rail

STAGE	LOCATIONS	MILES
1	Chester – Waverton	4.4
2	Waverton – Beeston/Bunbury (A49)	8.6
3	A49 – Barbridge	4.7
4	Barbridge – Nantwich	6.0
5	Nantwich – Hough	6.9
6	Hough – Audley	7.3
7	Audley – Bradwell (A34)	3.5
8	Bradwell A34 – Stoke	7.8
9	Stoke – Tittensor	6.8
10	Tittensor – Stone	4.9
11	Stone – Sandon	4.9
12	Sandon – Stafford	6.3
13	Stafford – Milford	4.6
14	Milford – Flaxley Green (A460)	6.5
15	Flaxley Green – Cannock Wood	3.2
16	Cannock Wood – Lichfield	5.8

TRANSPORT LINKS

D. Jones & Son C56 towards Chester or 41A or 41B

Infrequent services in this area include D&G 55 (Mon – Fri), GHA 56 (Thurs & Sat) GHA 83 Tue) or walk two miles from Wharton's Lock to the A51 at Tarporley for Arriva North West 84

Arriva North West 84 to Nantwich or Chester

BR, Arriva North West 84 towards Crewe & several other options

D&G Bus 44 & 44A towards Crewe or Nantwich

Arriva North West 34 to Hanley via Newcastle and 94, 94A towards Newcastle

Arriva North West 84 towards Crewe First 20 towards Hanley
Baker's Buses/Coaches Guide issue 94A towards Newcastle

First Potteries Ltd 17 towards Newcastle then
First Potteries Ltd 26 towards Hanley Br BR 300 yards from bridge 113 on canal

First Potteries Ltd/101 towards Stafford or Hanley

First Potteries Ltd/101 towards Stafford or Hanley
BR to Stafford, Stoke or Crewe

Baker's Buses/Coaches Guide issue X1 towards Hanley or Stafford Hospital

BR. First Potteries Ltd 101 towards Stone and Hanley
Arriva Midland North 825 towards Lichfield

Arriva Midland North 825 towards Stafford or Lichfield

Take the 32 to Rugeley and then the 825 towards Stafford

62A towards Lichfield
(from Hayfield Hill)

BR and many bus connections

Waymarking and Signage

The Two Saints Way is, as far as we know, the first to be signed by taking two motifs from the logo and using them to indicate the direction of travel.

If you are journeying from Chester to Lichfield you follow the **cross of St Chad** and if you are going from Lichfield to Chester you follow the **goose of St Werburgh**.

Where the route is straightforward and there is no possibility of confusion, simply follow the yellow arrows which are standard signage for public footpaths. The Two Saints Way is in places shared with other promoted routes.

Here are other signs for you to be aware of:

Between Shrewbridge Road (just south of Nantwich) and Weston, the Two Saints Way joins the Crewe and Nantwich Circular, so follow those signs except where it leaves that route near Wybunbury which will be clearly indicated by signage and in this guidebook.

From Milford across Cannock Chase to Gentleshaw Common the Two Saints Way will follow the Heart of England Way, so look out for the distinctive green oak tree discs there.

Other routes that join the Two Saints Way more briefly include the Sandstone Trail, the Weaver Way, the Newcastle Way, the Millennium Way and the Staffordshire Way.

Visiting Sites

Some places you may want to visit have limited opening hours and others can only be seen by permission of the owner. **If you wish to visit, it would be wise to make contact beforehand.** Here is a list of some of those sites:

St James' Christleton
Tel: 01244 335 663
www.christleton.org.uk/christleton/stjames

Bunbury Mill
Tel: : 01829 733 244
peter.robinson@bunburymill.com

Englesea Brook Chapel and Museum
Tel: 01270 820 836
www.engleseabrook-museum.org.uk/visitor.asp

Holy Trinity Church, Chesterton
Tel: 01782 562 479 (Simon Boxall)
www.holytrinitychesterton.org.uk

City Central Mosque, Stoke
Tel: 01782 204 092
citycentralmosque.org

Etruria Museum, Stoke
Mob: 07900 267 711
info@etruriamuseum.org.uk

Stoke Minster
Tel: 01782 747 785
office@stokeminster.org
www.stokeminster.org

St Dominic's, Stone
Tel: 01785 812 091

St Michael & St Wulfad, Stone
Mob: 07866 341 111 (Dennis Abbott)
dennis.abbott4@gmail.com

The Priory, Stone
Tel: 01785 818 688 (Timothy Gillow)
thegillows@yahoo.co.uk

Aston Hall, south of Stone
Tel: 01785 812 001 (Deacon Trevor)

St Chad's Stafford
Tel: 01785 245 450
(Andrew Baker)
www.stchadsstafford.co.uk

St Thomas Priory Farm, nr Stafford
Mr John Martin:
email dfoss@metronet.co.uk
or phone 01785 223 748

Beaudesert Park, Cannock Chase
Email info@beaudesert.org
or phone 01543 682 278

Reflection Gardens, Cannock Wood
www.reflectiongardens.org.uk
John & Christine Polhill:
email polhill@reflectiongardens.org.uk
or phone 01543 674 474

Additional Advice and the Countryside Code

Here are some other things you should bear in mind before you set out...

- **Muddy footpaths.**
  We are seeking to keep paths in a reasonable condition, but after heavy rain some sections may become very muddy. There are usually minor roads close by and where we know it can get muddy, we have indicated a road alternative.

- **Footpath changes.**
  We recommend you visit **http://www.twosaintsway.co.uk/path-updates.html** before your walk for any updates or changes which may have taken place since the guide was published. Please report any footpath issues you encounter to Marg Hardcastle at marg.twosaintsway@icloud.com

- **Walking on roads.**
  Most of the route is on footpaths but occasionally minor roads are used. Near Lichfield we use Cross in Hand Lane which was walked by pilgrims in the Middle Ages. This route is generally quiet, but it would be best to avoid rush hour. Please keep to the right-hand side of the road except when you come to a right-hand bend in which case cross carefully to the left-hand side about 100 yards beforehand and then return to the right-hand side.

- **Please keep to the Countryside Code – see below.**

The Countryside Code

On the Two Saints Way, follow the Countryside Code at all times:

- Guard against all risk of fire.
- Leave all gates as you find them.
- Use stiles when provided.
- Keep dogs under close control.
- Keep to paths across farmland.
- Avoid damaging fences, hedges and walls.
- Leave no litter of any kind.
- Safeguard water supplies.
- Protect wildlife, plants and trees.
- Go carefully on country roads.
- Respect the life of the countryside.
- Take only photographs, leave only footprints.

THE STORY OF THE TWO SAINTS WAY

The idea for the Two Saints Way came to me soon after my wife Pam and I came to Stone in the autumn of 2007. I quickly became intrigued by the foundational story of the town which is the legend of the two princes St Wulfad and St Rufin. There is a summary of the legend on page 74. It is significant that this story features both St Chad and St Werburgh. I noted that apart from various sites in Stone itself, there were other places in the Trent Valley between Trentham and Salt that had connections with the legend, such as the Saxon hill fort at Bury Bank (formerly called Wulpherecestre) and St Rufin's Church in Burston. Initially I conceived the idea of linking together these sites into a story trail between Trentham and Stafford.

In late 2008, two significant conversations extended this idea into a full pilgrimage route. Firstly, Stafford's chief librarian Andrew Baker suggested that it would be possible to extend the story trail from Stafford to Lichfield over Cannock Chase along the Heart of England Way. This seemed highly appropriate as Lichfield Cathedral had housed the shrine of St Chad. Later, I was in a meeting with Philip Morgan, senior lecturer in history at Keele, and he pointed out that a pilgrimage route existed between Chester Cathedral and Lichfield Cathedral. From there many pilgrims would have continued to Canterbury or even further to Rome or Jerusalem. When I realised that Chester was where the shrine of St Werburgh was located, I began to consider the possibility of linking up existing paths to create a revived pilgrimage route between the cities.

David Pott © Teeranlall Ramgopal

At this point, the venture was called the St Chad's Way Project. I then began to make connections with various potential partners and during 2009 a support group was formed and then later a steering group. The focus of my research had been the Mercian and Anglo-Saxon heritage and along the proposed route, I discovered Saxon stones at Acton near Nantwich and at Chesterton, as well as Saxon preaching crosses at Stoke Minster and Trentham. The discovery of the Staffordshire Hoard in July 2009 was highly significant for the project as it greatly increased interest in Mercian heritage. The Hoard has been dated at the same period as St Chad and St Werburgh in the 7th century.

The steering group met regularly from the spring of 2010, under the chairmanship of Dr Teeranlall Ramgopal, Pro-Vice Chancellor of Staffordshire University.

Members also included representatives from both cathedrals, British Waterways and the tourist boards.

Chester Cathedral quite rightly wanted equal honour for St Werburgh and in June 2010 the present name of The Two Saints Way was adopted.

In January 2011, The Two Saints Way Project was set up as a company limited by guarantee - company no 7483349. The inaugural pilgrimage of The Two Saints Way took place in the spring of 2012 and the signage of the route followed. In the autumn of 2015, the first edition of the guidebook was published.

A number of organisations have signed a partnership agreement with the Two Saints Way and several other organisations have also offered support. Here are some of our partners:

Lichfield Cathedral:
www.lichfield-cathedral.org

Chester Cathedral:
www.chestercathedral.com

Staffordshire University:
www.staffs.ac.uk

Stoke Minster:
www.stokeminster.com

Canal & River Trust:
http://canalrivertrust.org.uk

Lichfield District Council:
www.lichfielddc.gov.uk

Nantwich Town Council:
www.nantwichtowncouncil.gov.uk

Northumbria Community:
www.northumbriacommunity.org

Visit Stoke:
www.visitstoke.co.uk

Enjoy Staffordshire:
www.enjoystaffordshire.com

St Chad's Foundation Trust:
www.saintchads.org.uk

Marketing Cheshire:
www.marketingcheshire.co.uk

Who were the Two Saints?

In medieval times particular places became a magnet for pilgrims because they either were said to contain some important relics or because they were the burial place or shrine of a saint.

Chester and Lichfield were the resting places of St Werburgh and St Chad respectively. Both cities were therefore important in their own right as pilgrimage destinations and they were also stopping places for those going on pilgrimages to such places as Holywell or Bardsey Island in Wales, or those travelling to Canterbury. Some even travelled as far as Rome and Jerusalem.

These two saints were key figures who lived at about the same time in the 7th century and who, by their labours, brought about a complete change in the religious and cultural landscape of Mercia. Between the 7th and 10th centuries Mercia was a powerful kingdom, occupying a somewhat larger area than the Midlands today and including, at its greatest extent, all of England south of the Dee and the Humber, and north of the Avon and the Thames.

Up to the last quarter of the 7th century, Mercia was still largely pagan but Christianity was reaching into Mercia from two different directions and with differing emphases. What some have termed Celtic Christianity had spread from Ireland via Iona to Lindisfarne in Northumbria through such personalities as St Columba and St Aidan. The kind of Christianity that was based in Canterbury in Kent was more deeply influenced by Rome. We shall soon see that our two saints were influenced by both these strands but there was certainly no evidence of a competitive or divisive spirit in either of them.

Walking near Barthomley © Candice Smith

St Werburgh

St Werburgh was the daughter of the Mercian King Wulphere and his wife Ermenild who was a princess from Kent. She may have been born at Bury Bank (formerly Wulpherecestre) near Stone.

Under the influence of her mother she learned the Christian faith from the Roman perspective and developed a pious and virtuous nature. She was very beautiful and attracted many admirers but she refused them, declaring that she wished to be married only to Christ. She eventually managed to persuade her father to allow her to enter a convent.

When the time came, she was escorted in great state to the Abbey of Ely where she was welcomed by her aunt Ethelreda, the abbess. Werburgh fell on her knees and asked that she might be received as a novice. She was stripped of her coronet and her royal garments, exchanging them for the veil and rough habit of a nun.

She made good progress and eventually she came to supervise all the convents in Mercia which became models of monastic discipline. Through the wealth of her family she also established new convents at Weedon in Northamptonshire, Hanbury in Staffordshire and some say at Trentham on our route. The original references mention Triccingham or Trytenham and most historians now believe that this convent was at Threckingham in Lincolnshire. However, some connection with Trentham so close to her childhood home cannot be discounted.

St Werburgh lived to a ripe old age and is said to have visited all her convents for farewell visits before her death in the 7th century. She was buried at Hanbury, but her body was later transferred to Repton. Around 875, a Danish army invaded, so it was deemed wise to transfer her remains to the walled burgh of Chester where her body was re-interred at the Saxon church of St Peter and St Paul. This church was rededicated to St Werburgh and St Oswald in 907 by Aethelflaed, daughter of King Alfred the Great. In due course Werburgh's shrine there became a major pilgrimage site and eventually the abbey church became Chester Cathedral.

Goose misericord from cathedral

The cult of St Werburgh continued to develop during the course of the Middle Ages and she was looked upon as the perfect model of Christian womanhood. Here is a short section extolling her virtues from a very long poem about St Werburgh written in 1521 by a monk in Chester called Henry Bradshaw.

Obseruynge the doctryne / of our lorde Ihesu,
Had his commaundymentes / in her herte full tru;
So that no creature / more perfyte myght be
In vertuous gyftes (by grace) than she.
She was replete / with gyftes naturall:
Her vysage moost pleasaunt / fayre and amyable,
Her goodly eyes / clerer than the crystall,
Her countenaunce comly / swete and commendable;
Her herte lyberall / her gesture fauourable.
She, lytell consyderynge / these gyftes transytory,
Set her felycyte / in chryst perpetually.
She hadde moche worshyp / welthe / and ryches,
Vestures / honoures / reuerence and royalte;
The ryches she dysposed / with great mekenesse
To the poore people / with great charyte.

The symbol of the goose associated with St Werburgh has its roots in a story told by the Flemish monk Goscelin. Some wild geese had ravaged her fields at Weedon, so as a punishment she shut the large flock indoors overnight. However being of a kindly disposition, she pardoned and released them the next morning. The geese soon discovered that one of their number was missing, having been stolen by a servant, so they came winging noisily back to Werburgh. She grasped the meaning of their clamour, and, having secured the release of the goose, she rejoiced with them, saying, 'Birds of the air, bless the Lord!' The whole flock then flew away and never again interfered with the land of the blessed Werburgh!

A 12th-century historian summed up her influence:

And so the merits of this maid are told at Chester, and her miracles extolled. Yet though she be generous and swift to answer all men's prayers, yet most gracious is her footfall among the women and boys, who pray as it might be to a neighbour and a woman of their own countryside.

NB There are no contemporary records about St Werbergh. The main source of information here is from a Life written by the Flemish monk Goscelin in Canterbury in the late 10th century.

17

St Chad

Most of what we know about St Chad comes from the writings of Bede who had a very high regard for him and who gathered information about him from those who knew Chad personally.

It seems most likely that Chad was born around 634 into a family of Northumbrian nobility, suggesting an Anglo-Saxon background. However, his name, which means 'battle' was popular in Wales and so it is possible he had a mixed ethnic background. He was one of four brothers, the others being Cedd, Cynibil and Caelin. It seems most likely that he was the youngest of the four.

As a young man he had his early training under St Aidan on the holy island of Lindisfarne. Aidan was said, like Christ, to have chosen twelve disciples including St Chad to especially train in evangelism. Aidan was Irish and the Celtic Christian influences on Chad were strengthened by further training in Ireland itself. He travelled with a companion called Egbert who later commented that Chad 'followed the monastic life together very strictly – in prayers and continence, and in meditation on Holy Scripture'.

While Chad was in Ireland, his older brother Cedd had become a prominent figure in the church. He was involved in missionary work in East Anglia and then established a monastic settlement at Lastingham on the Yorkshire Moors. He contracted the plague, and just before he died in 664, he requested that his brother Chad should take over his position. Chad did so and returned from Ireland to take up his new post. He gained a reputation there for his wise leadership and the warmth of his hospitality.

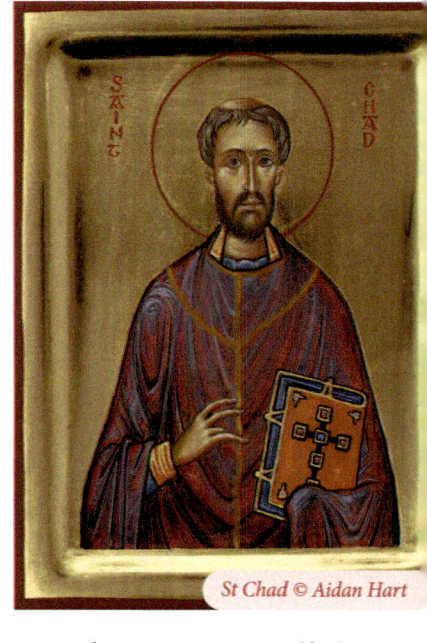

St Chad © Aidan Hart

In 665 the pro-Roman St Wilfred was expected to become Bishop of York but he left the country to seek a valid ordination in France as some considered ordinations in Britain to be invalid. In his absence King Oswiu of Northumbria became impatient for religious guidance in his kingdom and sent Chad to Kent to be ordained Bishop of the Northern Church at York.

Chad took to his new task with characteristic zeal and was well known for refusing to ride on horseback, preferring to walk in order to engage more easily with people as he preached the gospel in the towns and countryside.

When St Wilfred returned in 666 he was displeased and opposed St Chad's ordination. Three years later a new Archbishop of Canterbury, Theodore of Tarsus, was appointed. He soon charged Chad with holding his office illegally. Chad quickly replied that if this were the case, he was very happy to resign as he had only taken up the bishopric out of a sense of duty and never thought himself worthy of the position. Theodore was so moved by Chad's humility that he promptly completed Chad's ordination in the Roman manner, but Chad preferred to resign and retired to Lastingham.

Soon after, a need arose for a new Bishop of Mercia. Theodore asked Chad to take on the responsibility, which he did in 669. Historically, there had been much hostility between Mercia and Northumbria and it would have been a challenge for Chad as a Northumbrian to take this position in Mercia. However, although he was only in office for three years, his ministry appears to have been highly effective. His humility and godliness were well known and he brought many to the faith. He is reputed to have baptised them in the well now called St Chad's Well by St Chad's Church in Lichfield. Legend also reports that he spent long hours standing in the well in prayer!

Chad died on 2nd March 672 and was buried in the church of St Mary. He was immediately venerated as a saint and his relics were soon taken to the Cathedral Church of St Peter. They were moved in the early years of the 14th century to a splendid marble shrine adorned with gold and precious stones. The shrine, which was originally made in Paris, was provided by Bishop Walter Langton. By 1378, the shrine was housed near the new Lady Chapel. At the time of the Reformation, the Bishop of Lichfield pleaded with Henry VIII to spare the shrine. This was done, but only for a short time. At some unknown date the head and some other bones were separated from the main shrine. Some of these bones were hidden over the centuries by Catholic families in Staffordshire and were found at Aston Hall which is on the Two Saints Way. They are now in the Roman Catholic Cathedral of Birmingham.

The origin of the distinctive St Chad's Cross come from a so-called carpet page in an 8th-century Mercian illuminated Gospel Book called the Gospels of St Chad. It is thought that this gospel was associated with the shrine of St Chad in the same way that the Lindisfarne Gospels were associated with the shrine of St Cuthbert. The Gospels of St Chad are in Lichfield Cathedral Library. There are 33 ancient churches and several wells dedicated to St Chad, mainly in the Midlands, as well as several modern dedications.

Connecting Medieval and Contemporary Pilgrimage

Of Stone: The venerable queen [Ermenild, mother of Wulfad and Rufin] had a finely constructed church built of stones in the same place ... After this, a multitude of the infirm and those suffering from diverse weaknesses and of others seeking God ... was accustomed to visit the place and to carry stones thither to the building. Whence that place is called Stanes. (Hugh Candidus)

Pilgrimage was a major feature of life in medieval England. It is recorded that in the 13th century, so many pilgrims were visiting the shrine of St Chad at Lichfield that they disrupted the normal services.

Why did people go on pilgrimage? One of the main reasons, as the quote above indicates, was to seek healing. Places like Chester, Lichfield and Stone became places of pilgrimage because of their association with a saint and because healing miracles were reported to have happened there. Obviously healing for specific ailments was often sought after, but there were also many able-bodied pilgrims who would be seeking healing in a broader understanding of the term. Pilgrimage offered a time for reflection and the opportunity to seek resolution of troubling issues in their lives. They journeyed to heal the sickness of the soul and realign their lives with the purposes of God.

One type of pilgrimage was known as penitential pilgrimage. Some offenders undertook this voluntarily, but others were sentenced to go on pilgrimage. For instance, there are records from the church courts at Tarvin near Chester which state that some people were sentenced to go on pilgrimage to Lichfield for the sin of fornication. This was perhaps an early form of restorative justice in which the offender, having had time to reflect on his misdeeds during his journey, would be restored back into his community.

For others the motivation would have been simply the appeal of something different and more adventurous than the daily grind and sameness of their lives. A pilgrimage was often the only time that a person left the confines of their own locality and presented the opportunity for them to broaden their horizons.

After its heyday in medieval times, pilgrimage declined, especially in northern Europe as a consequence of the Reformation, but in recent years there has been a marked increase in the popularity of pilgrimage routes. In 1984 a mere 2,491 walked the famous Camino to Santiago de Compostela in Spain, but in 2010 over 270,000 pilgrims made the journey. In the UK, a number of pilgrimage routes have been revived and new ones have been set up in recent years, routes such as St Cuthbert's Way, St Oswald's Way the Cistercian Way and the North Wales Pilgrim Way which starts only 18 miles away from the Two Saints Way at Holywell. While there has been a decline in churchgoing in the last hundred years in the West, there is a new enthusiasm for what is perceived as the more active spirituality of pilgrimage.

While not all those who walk on new pilgrimage routes are spiritually motivated, there are ways in which the motivations of medieval pilgrims can be applied in the contemporary context. There is a growing interest in the concept of well-being and there can be few better ways of seeking well-being in its broadest sense, embracing physical, emotional, relational and spiritual health, than to embark on a pilgrimage. As medieval pilgrims journeyed to seek healing, even so, modern-day pilgrims on the Two Saints Way may, if they so choose, venture forth with the intention of making a journey of discovery and reconnection and in so doing, finding health in body, mind and soul.

A meditation guide for pilgrims is available on request.

THE CATHEDRAL CITIES   Chester

Chester, The Cross © Joe Wainwright

A brief history

Chester was founded by the Romans who built a large fort there called Deva Victrix in AD 79.

Chester's four main roads, Eastgate Street, Northgate Street, Watergate Street and Bridge Street, still follow the pattern laid down 2,000 years ago. Two significant Roman features that can still be seen are the amphitheatre, which could seat up to 10,000 people, and the Minerva shrine which is the only rock-cut Roman shrine still in its original location in Britain. After the Roman army left in the 5th century, a Romano-British civilian population remained.

Early in the 7th century, the Northumbrians captured the city after the gruesome Battle of Chester. The inhabitants called their city Legacaestir – the city of the Legions. The Welsh name Caerleon had the same meaning. The shortened forms of Chester and Caer developed during the Middle Ages.

Chester was the last town in England to be captured by the Normans. William the Conqueror ordered the castle to be built and Chester was always a key location for the domination of Wales.

Chester has some fine medieval timber-framed buildings and although a number of the black and white buildings in the centre are Victorian reconstructions, many of the internal features date back to the 13th century. The city walls, which are almost complete, are some of the best preserved in England.

Chester was somewhat overshadowed in the early stages of the Industrial Revolution and as the River Dee silted up, Liverpool took over as the main port of the region. Later on however railways, canals and new roads were built leading to rapid expansion and development.

Much of the land in the city centre is owned by the Duke of Westminster. In the 19th century the Duke employed an architect called John Douglas who designed many prominent buildings including the Grosvenor Hotel and the City Baths.

In 2007 a ten-year plan, called Chester Renaissance, was initiated at a cost of £1.3 billion to develop the city as 'a must-see European destination'.

Chester as a pilgrimage city

In medieval times, Chester became a pilgrimage city on two counts. Firstly, St John's Church, the Mercian minster, became the city's first cathedral. It was believed to hold a piece of the true cross (the Holy Rood) and was much visited, in particular by Welsh pilgrims. Professor Catherine A.M. Clarke of the University of Southampton comments that 'many Welsh poems about Chester are satirical and hostile, reflecting the status of Chester as a colonialist city involved in the control and oppression of Wales. Yet the poems relating to the relics of the cross show that Chester had a very powerful spiritual pull – and the power of pilgrimage and spirituality to transcend political difference and division'.

The second reason why Chester developed as a pilgrimage site was of course because of the shrine of St Werburgh at the church which was dedicated to her. This abbey church became Chester's later cathedral under Henry VIII.

In the late 12th century, a monk from St Werburgh's wrote a book called *De Laude Cestrie (On the Glory of Chester)*. In it he writes of Chester as a holy city, spiritually significant in its basic structure:

Chester also has two perfectly straight streets intersecting like the blessed cross, which form four roads, culminating at the four gates, mystically revealing the marvellously innate grace of the Great King, who, through the four evangelists, showed the twin law of the old and new testaments to be completed through the mystery of the holy cross ... anyone standing in the the middle of the marketplace, may turn his face to the east and examine the position of the churches noting John, precursor of the Lord, in the east, Peter the apostle in the west, Werburgh the virgin in the north, and Michael the Archangel in the south. There is nothing truer than this verse: **Upon thy walls, O Jerusalem, I have appointed watchmen [Isa 62:6].** *Nothing is sweeter than this evidence that God gave us such guardians: it is a sacred offering and charming mystery. It comforts men's spirits and encourages contemplation.*

All this no doubt sounds fanciful to modern ears, but it surely provides a context for understanding the deep significance of Chester as a pilgrimage destination.

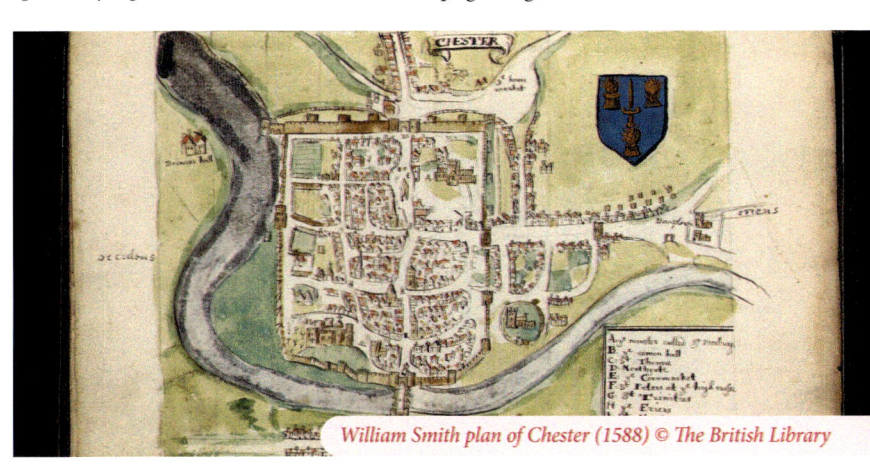

William Smith plan of Chester (1588) © The British Library

'Water of Life' by Stephen Broadbent © David Pott

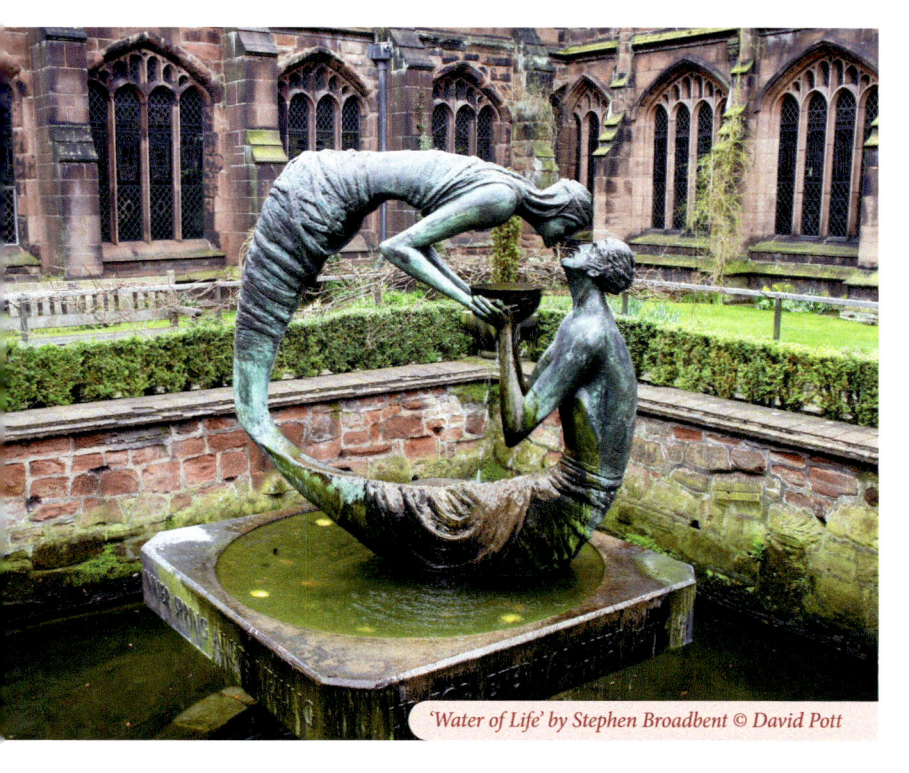

Chester Cathedral

On the site of the present cathedral, it is thought that Christian worship began in late Roman times in a basilica dedicated to St Paul and St Peter. The dedication changed to St Werburgh after her remains came to Chester in 907. At the same time a new church dedicated to St Peter was built at the Cross. Aethelfleda developed the chapel into a college of secular canons with an abbey, but this was destroyed and the canons were evicted in 1090.

Three years later, High Lupus, Earl of Chester, established a Benedictine monastery on the site: the earliest surviving parts of the building date from that time. During the Dissolution of the Monasteries in 1538, the shrine of St Werburgh was desecrated and the monastery closed, but by 1541 the church began its new life as Chester Cathedral and the dedication changed from St Werburgh to Christ and the Blessed Virgin Mary.

The cathedral, which is built of new red sandstone, is an amalgam of architectural styles, beginning with Norman in the north-west tower, north transept and monastic buildings. Much of the church, starting with the Lady Chapel, was rebuilt in the Gothic style in the 13th and 14th centuries. The cloister, central tower, south transept and large west window are in the Perpendicular style while the front of the west entrance is Tudor. The cathedral was extensively restored primarily by George Gilbert Scott in the 18th century.

Ruins at east end of St John's Church © David Pott

St John's Church

The church was founded as the great Saxon Minster of Mercia by King Aethelred in 689. In 1075 the Bishop of Lichfield moved the seat of his see to Chester and St John's became his cathedral until he died in 1085. Coventry then became the main cathedral for the large diocese, but St John's remained as a co-cathedral until the present cathedral was established in 1541.

Since then it has been a parish church. Large-scale building took place in the 12th and 13th centuries, but most of the east end was destroyed during the Dissolution of the Monasteries – some of the remains can be seen at the east end of the church. It is recognised as one of the finest examples in Europe of the transition from Romanesque style to the Gothic style.

The Nave at St John's Church © David Pott

THE CATHEDRAL CITIES — Lichfield

Lichfield © Angela Bickley

A brief history

In the first century AD, the Romans built a fort called Letocetum two miles south of the present city.

There is an ancient tradition that early Christians were martyred here, possibly during Diocletian's persecutions in the early 4th century. It is likely that a Celtic settlement continued in the area after the Romans left. In 669, the Venerable Bede records that St Chad established his bishopric at 'Licidfelth' which is said to mean 'Field of the Dead', possibly alluding to the early martyrs. Lichfield soon developed as the main ecclesiastical centre for Mercia.

In the Doomsday survey, Lichfield was listed as a village, but in the 12th century, Bishop Clinton fortified the cathedral close and laid out Lichfield on the ladder pattern which survives today. In 1387, Richard I gave a charter for the foundation of the Guild of St Mary and St John the Baptist and the guild functioned in local government until the town was incorporated by Edward VI in 1546.

Lichfield suffered greatly during the Civil War. It was a Royalist stronghold in a strategic location. The Parliamentarians captured it in 1643 and desecrated the cathedral. It was retaken for the Royalists by Prince Rupert, but surrendered once more in 1646. The town was restored by Bishop Hackett with funds partly provided by King Charles II.

The highpoint of Lichfield's history was in the 17th century, when it became a magnet for intellectuals such as Samuel Johnson, Erasmus Darwin, David Garrick and Anna Seward. It was known as 'a city of philosophers'. It grew in prosperity and was an important coaching station on the route to the north-west and Ireland.

As Birmingham grew during the Industrial Revolution, Lichfield's significance as a communications centre declined, but it generally retained its genteel character. In the latter part of the 20th century there was considerable expansion particularly to the east of the city centre and the population grew threefold. Today Lichfield is a popular tourist destination with much to offer the discerning visitor. Large areas of pools and parkland bring the countryside into the heart of the city.

Lichfield as a pilgrimage city

Such was the reputation of St Chad that soon after he died in 672, pilgrims began to flock to his tomb, which was on the site of the present St Chad's Church. A major reason for the building of the cathedral in 700 was to provide a more worthy shrine for visiting pilgrims. Lichfield could perhaps claim to be England's first pilgrim cathedral.

There are records of healing associated with the shrine including that of a madman who slept on the shrine and was restored to sanity by the time he awoke. Bede describes an interesting custom in relation to the shrine in this way:

The shrine of St Chad was a wooden coffin in the shape of a little house with an aperture in the side through which the devout can ... take out some of the dust, which they put into water and give to sick cattle or men to drink, upon which they are presently eased of their infirmity and restored to health.

St Chad's shrine was not the only place of pilgrimage in Lichfield. Pilgrims also visited St Chad's Well by St Chad's Church close to where his body originally rested. The waters were reputed to have healing powers and were used for bathing.

By the time of the Middle Ages, the crowds of pilgrims were bringing prosperity to Lichfield. St Chad's Day, 2nd March, was a highlight in the pilgrim calendar when the cathedral was decorated with colourful wall hangings and bells rang out as the bones of the saint were carried around in procession. At times their numbers were so great that the regular services were being disrupted. This may have been the motivation for the building of the Lady Chapel beyond the Choir. Here Bishop Langton paid £2,000 for a magnificent new shrine.

By the 15th century, the bones had been separated and his head was preserved in a reliquary in the St Chad's Head Chapel above the south aisle.
This all came to an end at the time of the Dissolution of the Monasteries when the shrine was destroyed. The bones of the saint were smuggled away and eventually found in a box at Aston Hall near Stone. From here they were taken to the new Roman Catholic Cathedral in Birmingham.

Some people have assumed that the unique pedilavium in the cathedral was used to wash the feet of pilgrims at the end of their journeys. It is just possible that this may have occurred but its main use was to wash the feet of the poor on Maundy Thursday. This custom was revived by pilgrims on the inaugural pilgrimage when they arrived at the end of their journey along the Two Saints Way.

Footwashing at Lichfield © Paul Graetz

For today's pilgrim, there are plenty of reminders of St Chad in the cathedral. For instance, in the Chapter House are two outstanding artefacts: the St Chad Gospels and the Lichfield Angel and in the St Chad's Head Chapel, restored in 1897, Chad's story is told in roundels that feature within the Minton tile decoration in the Choir.

In 1972, to commemorate the 1300th anniversary of St Chad's death, a plaque was erected in the Lady Chapel where the shrine had existed before the Reformation and this has become the main focal point.

It is quite possible that the St Chad Gospels once adorned the shrine of St Chad. This 8th-century manuscript, written on 118 leaves or folios (thus 236 pages), comprises the Gospels of Matthew and Mark and the beginning of Luke's Gospel. There are eight illuminated pages. For a time in the 9th and 10th centuries, the St Chad Gospels were located in Wales (possibly for safe keeping from Viking raiders) and they contain inscriptions which are the earliest known writings in Welsh. By 1020, it is known that the Gospels were back in Lichfield and there they have remained apart from a brief period during the Civil War.

The Lichfield Angel is an exquisite two-foot-tall limestone carving which was discovered in 2003 when the nave was being excavated prior to the installation of a new platform. It is very possible that this also had a direct connection with St Chad and formed an end to the chest which housed his remains. It is likely that the angel is Gabriel and that the carving is part of an Annunciation scene where Mary would have featured in the other part. The carving is of a very high quality and the lack of weathering means that much of the colouring is still in place.

Lichfield Angel © Lichfield Camera Club

Lichfield Cathedral © David Keith Jones

Lichfield Cathedral

This cathedral, with its three distinctive spires called 'the 'Ladies of the Vale', is dedicated to St Chad and St Mary. The central spire is 250 feet high. The basic construction is of sandstone from a quarry to the south of the city.

The first Saxon cathedral was built in AD 700, but was replaced in the late 11th century by a Norman cathedral. Some stonework from that period can be found in the Consistory Court. The substance of what we see today is the Gothic cathedral of the 13th century, including the Choir (1200), the octagonal Chapter House (1249) and the Nave (1260).

The cathedral suffered greatly from the ravages of the Reformation and from the Civil War. It is because of this that most of the forest of statues on the fine 14th-century West Front are of Victorian origin.

A special treasure is the Herkenrode Glass in the Lady Chapel. It is recognised as the greatest collection of 16th-century Flemish stained glass in the world. It was obtained in 1801 when the Belgian Abbey at Herkenrode was dissolved. The glass has been restored at a cost of £3.7million

The Victorian architect Sir George Gilbert Scott was responsible for a sensitive restoration of the cathedral to its medieval splendour between 1855 and 1878.

STAGE 1 Chester to Waverton 4.4 miles

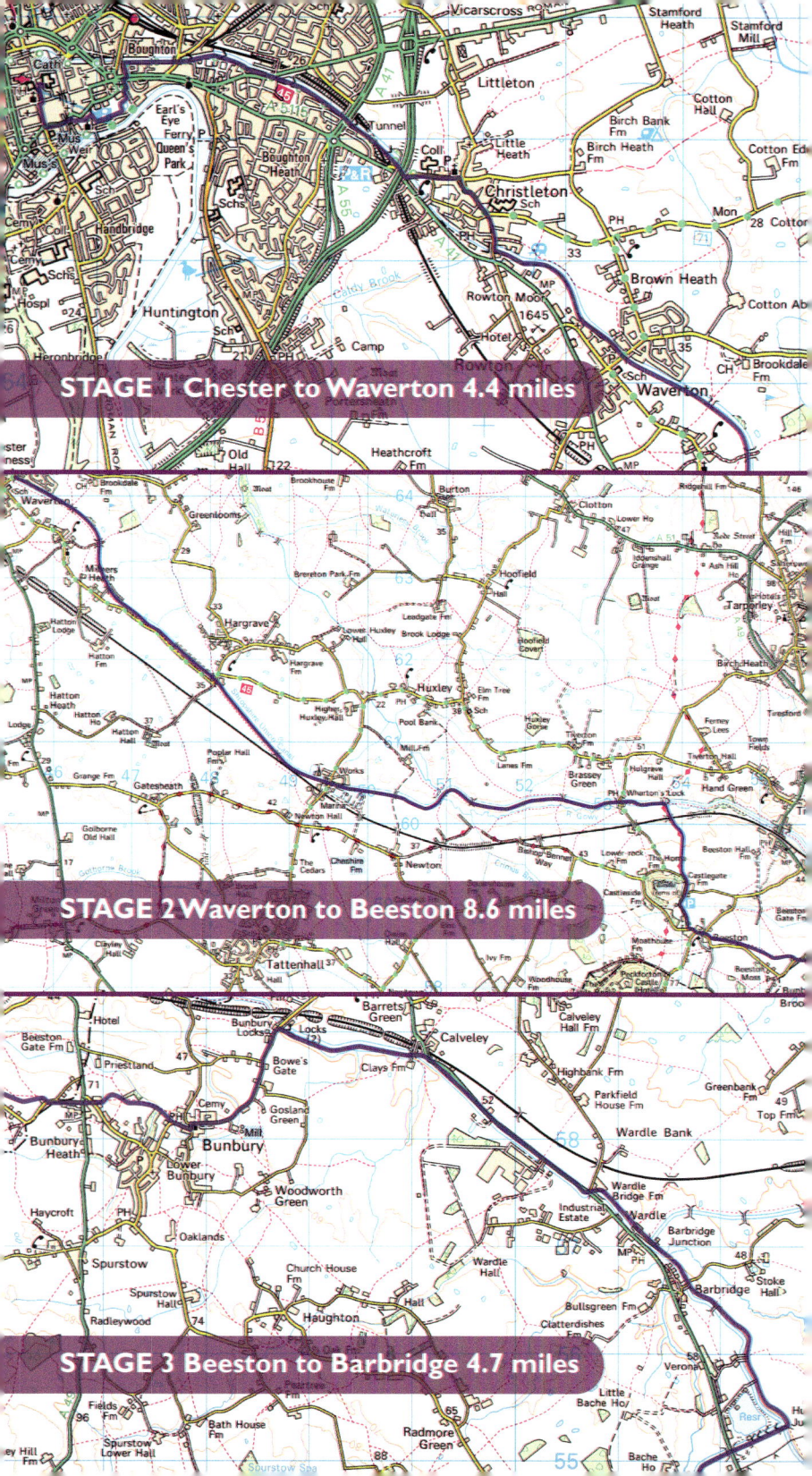

STAGE 2 Waverton to Beeston 8.6 miles

STAGE 3 Beeston to Barbridge 4.7 miles

STAGE 4 Barbridge to Nantwich 6 miles

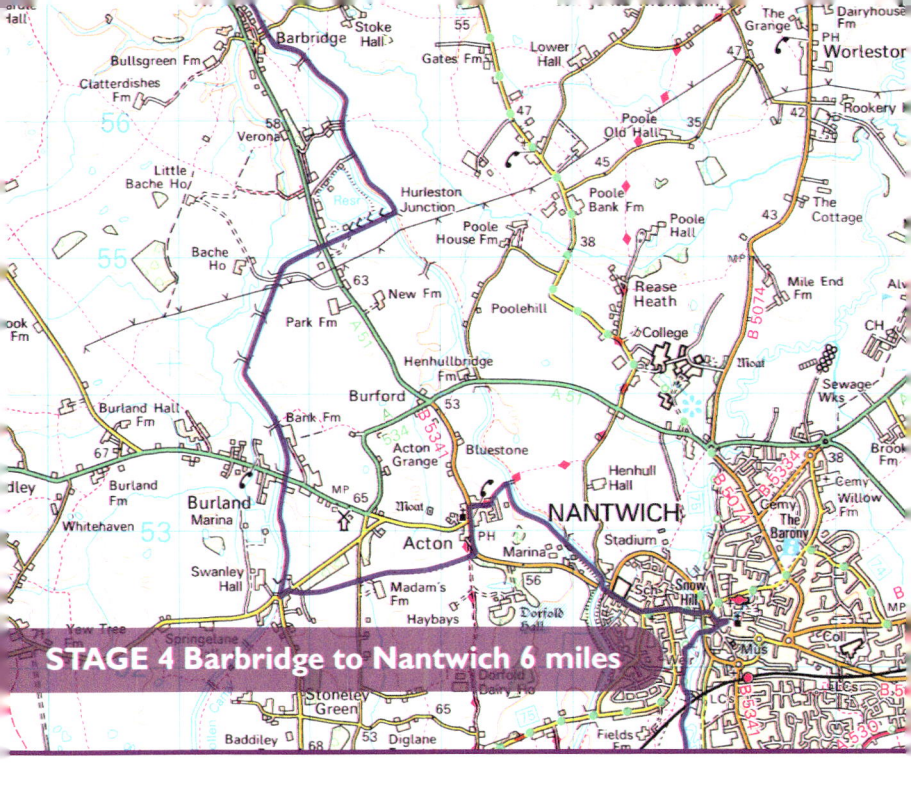

EXPLANATION OF SIGNS

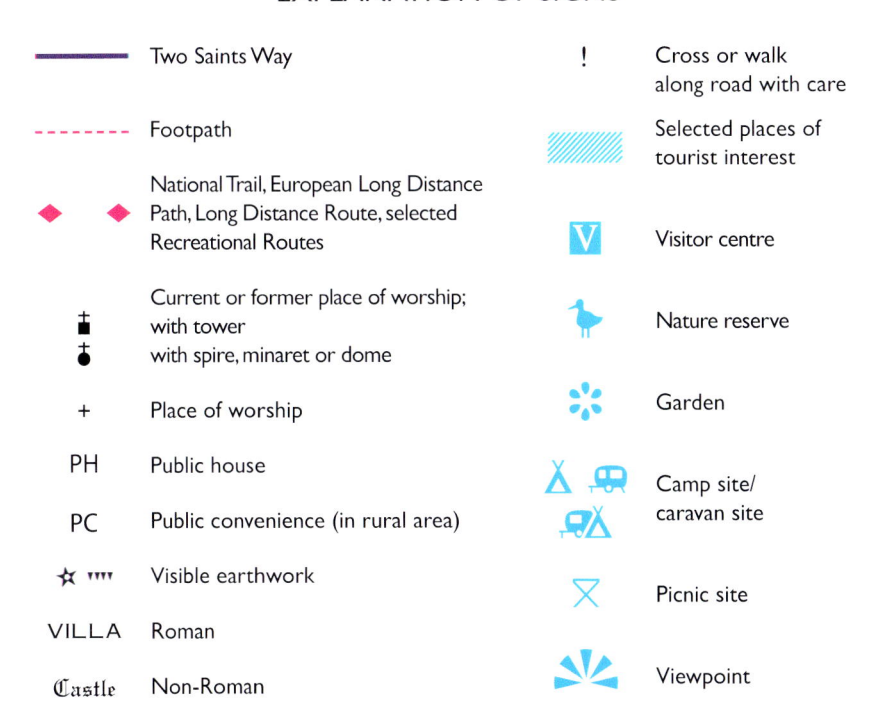

———	Two Saints Way
- - - - -	Footpath
♦ ♦	National Trail, European Long Distance Path, Long Distance Route, selected Recreational Routes
╪ / ♦	Current or former place of worship; with tower / with spire, minaret or dome
+	Place of worship
PH	Public house
PC	Public convenience (in rural area)
☆ ⊥⊥⊥⊥	Visible earthwork
VILLA	Roman
Castle	Non-Roman
!	Cross or walk along road with care
▧	Selected places of tourist interest
V	Visitor centre
🐦	Nature reserve
✻	Garden
⛺ 🚐	Camp site/ caravan site
⌛	Picnic site
☀	Viewpoint

SECTION 1 Chester to Nantwich 23.5 miles

Your journey begins at the shrine of St Werburgh in Chester Cathedral. After you have completed your visit and walked out of the cathedral at the visitors' entrance, turn right into St Werburgh Street. The Gothic-style town hall is ahead of you. Turn left and walk down Northgate Street. At the bottom of the street turn right to the Cross standing beside St Peter's Church. This is the central ancient crossroads of the city. Turn left down Bridge Street. Half way down on the left hand side at no.39 is Spudulike. This is well worth a visit to experience the incongruity of a fast food restaurant juxtaposed with the perfectly preserved section of the Roman baths and hypocaust system in the basement!

Continue down Bridge Street. When you come to the crossroads, turn left into Pepper Street. Keep on the left-hand side and pass through the rounded arch of Newgate. This was formerly called the Wolf Gate or Wulfad's Gate – perhaps because the next major destination for medieval pilgrims was the shrine of St Wulfad at Stone. Continue to the lights and cross over to the other side towards

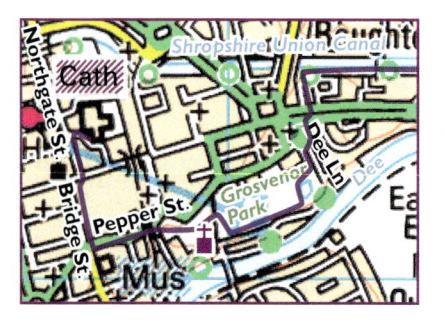

Shrine of St Werburgh © David Pott

the Roman amphitheatre. Turn right and then left to cross over the ramp at the amphitheatre to arrive at St John's Church.

After visiting St John's, turn right and walk round the north and eastern sides of the church before entering Grosvenor Park where you continue along the central avenue between the high shapely holly bushes to the white statue of the Second Marquis of Westminster who donated the park to the city in 1867. Turn left here. Take the next right past the pond and exit the park turning left into Dee Lane. Cross over the dual carriageway (Boughton) at the lights and go right, then immediately left into Russell Street. You soon reach the canal where you turn right along the towpath.

STAGE 1 Chester to Waverton 4.4 miles

The Shropshire Union Canal and the Chester Canal

It was not until 1846 that the name of the Shropshire Union was first used: this was when the constituent canals were amalgamated to form the Shropshire Union Railways and Canal Company before being taken over by the London and North Western Railway Company.

The Chester to Nantwich section on the Two Saints Way, called the Chester Canal, is the oldest part of the system built between 1772 and 1779. The canal system that developed had a somewhat chequered history, but a major turning point was the link with the Ellesmere Canal in 1795. This created a more viable enterprise since it carried cargoes from North Wales and Shropshire to join with the Chester Canal at Hurleston near Nantwich, and then north from Chester on the Wirral Branch of the Ellesmere Canal to join the River Mersey at Netherpool (now known as Ellesmere Port). In the 1830s the Middlewich Branch linking with the Trent and Mersey Canal, and the line from Nantwich to Autherley to the Staffordshire & Worcestershire Canal were also completed. The new access to Liverpool, Manchester, The Potteries and Birmingham meant that the canals became even more profitable. Over the following decades as other canal systems declined, the Shropshire Union continued to prosper, largely because of subsidies from the LWNR – the number of narrowboats grew from 213 in 1870 to 395 in 1889 and by 1902 there were 450. After World War I, however, subsidies ceased and the pattern of heavy losses led to closures. In recent times it has been restored to full working order.

Shropshire Union Canal © Candice Smith

SECTION 1 Chester to Nantwich 23.5 miles

As you start your journey along the canal, you soon come to Hoole Lane Lock. On the opposite side is a small chapel with an attractive little spire, now converted into houses. This was a chapel of ease for St Paul's Church Boughton, called St Paul's Mission, and it was probably used as an outreach to boatmen and their families. Just past the Water Tower is Chemistry Lock. A factory here in the 19th century produced naphtha, hence the name of the area.

The next lock is Tarvin Road with its characteristic lock cottage and unusual circular Lengthsman's Hut, one of three still in existence on the Chester Canal. Next you pass under the A41 (bridge no. 122B) and the canal then crosses over the railway. After passing under the A55 (no. 122A), go up onto the next bridge (no. 122) and turn left on the road into Christleton. Proceed past the law college along Pepper Street. You soon reach St James Church on your left.

St James' Christleton

Recent investigations suggest that a church existed on this site soon after the Roman occupation of Chester, and before the arrival of the pagan Saxons during the 7th century. The name Christleton means 'the place of Christians' and is the only place with this name in the world. It is almost certain that a more substantial wooden building existed by the 14th century and the present tower is thought to be from the second church, built in the time of Rector Thomas in 1484. It is said that a woodcutter, Thomas Mayor from Bavaria, was employed at this time and his descendants have worshipped here ever since. The church was in the patronage of the monks of the Abbey in Chester. Water from the Abbot's Well in Christleton was channelled in clay pipes through Boughton to the site of the Abbey (now Chester Cathedral).

During 1645 the church was occupied by soldiers from the Parliamentarian Army commanded by Sir William Brereton. In 1873 part of the roof of the Georgian brick building of 1736 collapsed and the congregation was covered in snow. The rebuild, featuring red and creamy white sandstone, was designed by William Butterfield and consecrated in July 1877.

The church contains many historic items including a bell tower with eight bells; stained glass windows by Charles Kempe & Co.; a font cut in Sicilian marble and fossil-rich Derbyshire limestone; a wooden carving of a pelican tearing open her breast to feed her young with her own blood; a Royal Coat of Arms dated 1665; an old village constable's staff; a Jacobean altar table; and a Millennium window depicting figures from the village life over the last 1,000 years.

STAGE 1 Chester to Waverton 4.4 miles

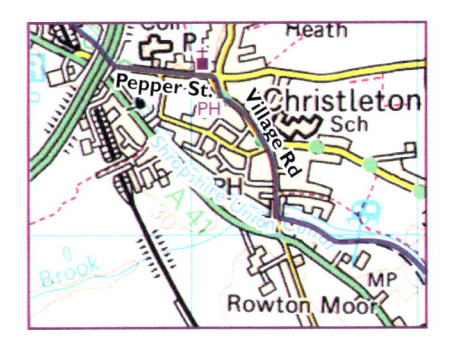

From the church, go down Village Road, passing the old Victorian Pump House, the well and village green. The Ring O Bells pub is on your right. Continue on to the end of Village Road until you see Christleton High School on your left. Continue straight across and along the narrower Rowton Bridge Road until you reach the canal. Go over the bridge and through the gate on your right. Turn right again under the bridge and continue along the towpath. On your right between here and the next village of Waverton is Rowton Moor which was the site of one of the last battles in the Civil War. It took place on 24th September 1645 and was decisively won by the Parliamentarians with 600 Royalists killed and 800 taken prisoner. Charles I is said to have watched the battle as it reached the suburbs of Chester from the Phoenix Tower (now King Charles' Tower) before fleeing to Denbigh.

The bridge at Waverton (no. 119) marks the end of the first stage.

St James Church © David Cummings

SECTION 1 Chester to Nantwich 23.5 miles

Continue along the towpath, with the spire of St Peter's Waverton prominent on the right. You now have a further six miles along the towpath before you will turn off for Beeston Castle. After you have passed bridge no. 112, the canal sweeps round to the left, where you cross an aqueduct over the River Gowy. You may like to slip down the steep path to take a look at the pedestrian tunnel under the canal. After this point, look out for barn owls which can sometimes be seen on the right-hand side where owl boxes have been installed by the Broxton Barn Owl Group. Next, you reach the Shady Oak pub where there is a campsite and soon after, you come to the next lock – Wharton's Lock. Here take the footpath on your right up to Beeston, cross a bridge and then proceed under the railway and on along the track until you reach the road circling the castle where you turn left. Pass Castlegate Farm on your left until you come to the entrance to Beeston Castle.

From the entrance to Beeston Castle, carry on down the hill to a T-junction where you turn left by an attractive timber-framed house into the village itself. Continue straight on, passing a road on your right to Peckforton and another on your left to Tiverton. As the road bends to the right, there is a footpath on the left which The Two Saints Way has formerly used, but as this is in dispute at the time of going to press, continue straight on along Moss Lane. There is a fork to the left which you ignore and you will soon reach the A49.

Beeston Castle

Beeston's crag is naturally defended on three sides and it is not surprising that it attracted prehistoric settlers who were followed by Bronze Age metalworkers. There was an immense Iron Age hill fort here which was adapted by the castle builders of the Middle Ages. Ranulf, Earl of Chester, a powerful baron under Henry III, began the 'Castle of the Rock' in the 1220s. The castle was subject to a long siege during the English Civil War, the Royalists eventually surrendering to the Parliamentarians in 1645.

The castle has a huge outer bailey and an inner bailey, defended on the hillside by a deep moat and a double-towered gatehouse. A distinctive feature of the inner bailey is the 328-foot-deep well, which is probably the deepest of any English castle. From this commanding location there are superb views on a clear day across eight counties and stretching from the Pennines in the east to the Welsh mountains to the west.

STAGE 2 Waverton to Beeston 8.6 miles

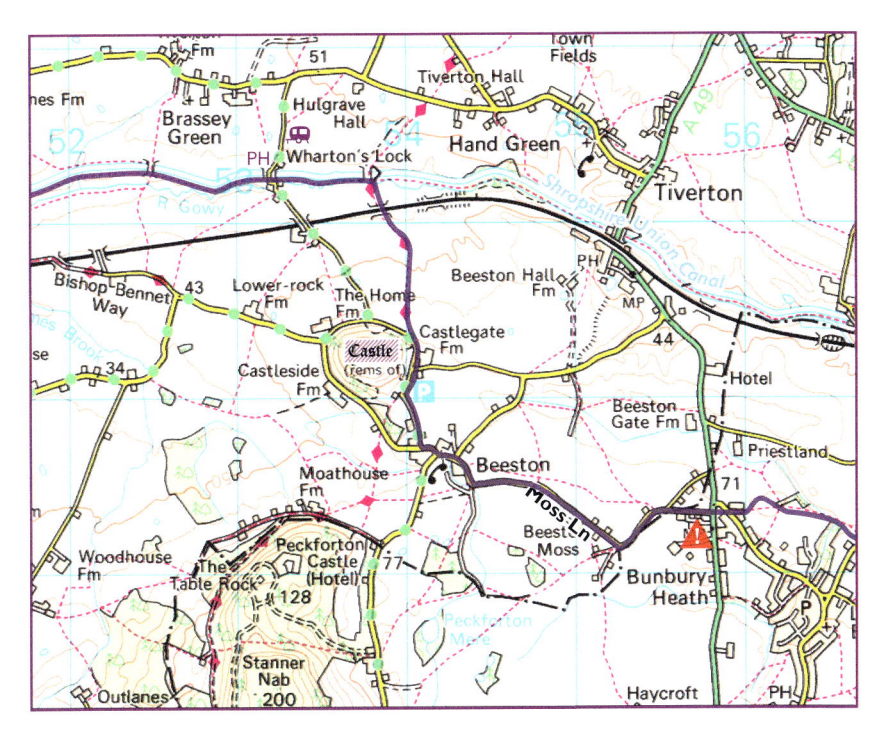

Beeston Castle © English Heritage

SECTION 1 Chester to Nantwich 23.5 miles

Cross over the A49 and go along School Lane for a few yards to a track on the left just past Woodside. Although unsigned, the track bears the name Wythin Street which can be seen later on the address plate of the last cottage. Follow this track down between Meadow View on your left and a timber-framed house on your right. Go through the kissing gate into the field. Cross towards a wood, keeping the field boundary to your left. The tower of Bunbury church is in view. Two footpaths leave to the left within a few yards of each other - take the second with the metal kissing gate, into a strip of woodland. Continue through a kissing gate, along the left edge of a field and then cross over a bridge before turning right with the impressive tower of the church now much closer. Walk to a gate which leads onto a road, turn left and go up to St Boniface Church, with the Dysart Arms opposite.

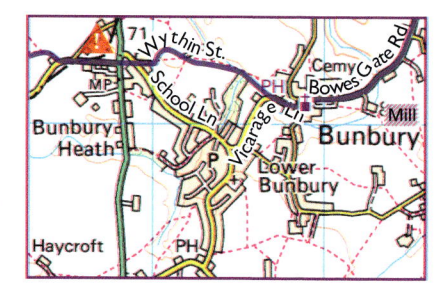

Bunbury

Bunbury is in fact a collection of four villages – Higher Bunbury, Lower Bunbury, Bunbury Heath and Bunbury Common – which have virtually become one. St Boniface Church stands at the high point. It is thought that a pagan site stood here before a wooden Anglo-Saxon church was built in the 8th century. A Norman church followed in the 11th century, but most of the present church was built as a collegiate church in the 14th century by Sir Hugh Calveley, whose alabaster tomb is in the church.

Opposite the church is a fine 18th-century pub, the Dysart Arms, named after the Tollemarche family who were also Earls of Dysart.

St James © David Pott

This image of St James in pilgrim garb can be found on the striking medieval parclose screen on the south wall of the church. It is located in the lower right hand corner of the painting of Salome.

STAGE 3 Beeston to Barbridge 4.7 miles

Bunbury Mill © Bunbury Watermill Trust

As you leave St Boniface Church, turn right round the church and exit the graveyard on to Bowe's Gate Road to take you back one mile to the canal. Take care along this stretch as there is no pavement beyond the village. You will pass an old mill on your right. The present mill dates from 1840; remarkably, it is still in full operation producing fine flour, as a heritage museum with a pleasant visitor centre. On arriving at the canal you will see Bunbury Locks. The two locks here are built as a staircase rising 15 feet 7 inches, and are the last ones on the Chester Canal before its terminus at Nantwich. The magnificent block of stables above the top lock used to have 22 stalls where the fast or 'fly' boats changed horses to enable them to keep up their high speed carriage of important and perishable cargoes.

After a further mile, you reach bridge no. 104 at Calveley where the towpath crosses from the south to the north side of the canal. The village was once quite a busy place with a number of cheese warehouses. It was an important place for transferring goods between canal boats and trains up until 1960. You can still find evidence that there was once a railway station here. Continue on for a further two miles. The canal runs parallel with the A51 on your left. You pass Wardle Industrial Estate on your right.

SECTION 1 Chester to Nantwich 23.5 miles

Barbridge Junction © Graham Dodd

Continuing on your way, you come to a bridge over the Middlewich Branch of the canal at Barbridge Junction. The canal at this point also follows the Weaver Way. At the village of Barbridge there is a notice welcoming pilgrims to visit the Methodist chapel. You may also like to cross the bridge (no. 100) to visit the Barbridge Inn on your right for refreshments. The stretch that follows between here and the canal junction at Hurleston is often very busy and has been called the 'Clapham Junction' of the inland waterways.

When you reach bridge no. 97 at Hurleston Junction, cross over to the Llangollen Canal, which begins with a wonderful ascent up four narrow locks. Hurleston Reservoir to the north of the locks has a capacity of 85 million gallons. It receives its water supply via the Llangollen Canal and in its turn supplies the Shropshire Union Canal as well as providing drinking water.

The Llangollen Canal

In 1791 an ambitious plan was devised to build the Ellesmere Canal, linking the Mersey with the Severn. The canal was initially successful as it provided an outlet to Liverpool for various cargoes such as coal, iron, other metals, limestone and grain which were transported mostly from North Wales. It also transported a good number of passengers. In 1846 the canal became part of the Shropshire Union network.

In 1936, after a breach on what is now the Montgomery Canal, traffic declined. Eventually, in 1944, the canal was effectively closed to navigation but was kept open as a water supply. With the rise of leisure use of canals in the latter part of the 20th century, the canal was restored as the Llangollen Canal and it is now one of the most popular in Britain.

STAGE 4 Barbridge to Nantwich 6 miles

Alternative routes

After passing under the A51, you may choose to make a diversion to Snugburys famous Jersey ice cream a quarter of a mile south at Park Farm. Snugburys is also famous for the huge straw sculptures that are made each year. After your visit, there is a footpath marked with white posts to lead you back to bridge no. 4 on the Llangollen Canal.

At bridge no. 6 at Burland, if it is very wet or you are short of time you may wish to walk east along the A534 and on at the junction into Monks Lane where you soon rejoin the main route at St Mary's Church. St Mary's was closely linked with Combermere Abbey – hence the name Monks Lane. There is a pavement all the way, but you would miss out on some attractive landscapes.

A peaceful walk along the canal follows. After 1.5 miles, you will pass Swanley Marina and a pipe bridge and just beyond the lock, leave the canal at the attractive Swanley Bridge (no 8). Cross over the road to Ravensmoor and continue into Swanley Lane. After 100 yards, take the footpath on your right and after crossing the stile go diagonally left to the corner of Long Plantation. Walk over two fields before crossing a minor road and on into an unmade road leading towards Madam's Farm.

Where the road bears right, the path goes straight ahead with an attractive line of birch trees on your right. This soon leads into a field. Cross this one and two more fields with good views of the impressive tower of St Mary's Acton which is your destination. Turn left at the path crossroads to join the A51.

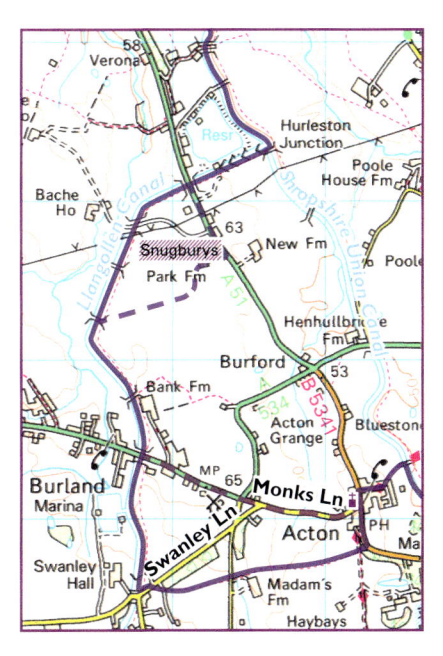

Pass the Star public house on your left and St Mary's Church is soon after on your left.

41

SECTION 1 Chester to Nantwich 23.5 miles

St Mary's Acton

There has been a place of worship here for a thousand years: Acton is much older than nearby Nantwich. Priests were recorded here in the Doomsday Book (1086). The oldest part of the present church is the tower that may be 900 years old and was sometimes used to shelter local inhabitants from Welsh raiders. The church expanded, especially in the 14th and 15th centuries and there have been three major restorations. During the last of these in 1897, some fine Anglo-Saxon stones were discovered, which can be found in the south aisle near the pulpit. In the churchyard are some 17th-century almshouses, reputedly the oldest brick buildings in south Cheshire, which are sadly in a dilapidated condition.

Saxon Stones © Charles Hull

Acton Church © Charles Hull

STAGE 4 Barbridge to Nantwich 6 miles

After visiting the church turn left and cross the A51. Then take the next turn on your right into Wilbraham Road. Before the road turns right, fork left to the footpath which soon leads to the canal. As you cross the bridge, pause to look at the interpretation board about the Civil War Battle of Nantwich which took place here in 1644. The footpaths sign here may initially seem a little confusing, but you need to go down to the canal and turn left under the bridge to continue towards Nantwich.

When you arrive at bridge no. 92 by the canal basin, you have reached the end of the old Chester Canal which was completed in 1794. It is still an important centre on the canal system. Continue on the left-hand side of the canal, built in 1834 as the Birmingham & Liverpool Junction Canal which carries on south to Wolverhampton. When the canal starts to swing round to the right, by the wooden statue of a dog, take the slip path down into Nantwich and cross over at the lights. Look back to enjoy the fine aqueduct by Thomas Telford before walking into the town along Welsh Row, passing Mallbank School and Sixth Form College on your left. There are several fine timber-framed houses, including Malthouse Cottage and, further on, Sir Roger Wilbraham's almshouses, now The Cheshire Cat. Continue straight over the River Weaver and the A534 into the High Street, **then take the next right to arrive at the town square and St Mary's Church..**

St Mary's Nantwich

Most of this red sandstone church was built in the 14th century. It is one of the finest medieval churches in England. The twenty canopied choir stalls are a priceless treasure with a wealth of carvings of great variety and charm.

The phrase 'parson's nose' may have originated with the carving of a previous vicar at the rear of the dodo like bird illustrated here!

More recent features include the superb kneelers, the Jubilee Curtain (1977) and the Creation Window depicting Cheshire farm life in conjunction with the Creation story. Note Halley's comet in the right trefoil - the window was made in 1985 when the comet appeared.

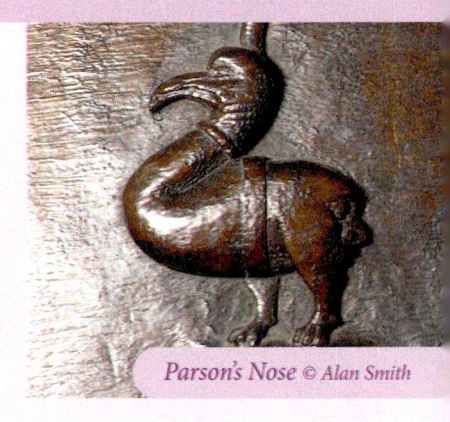

Parson's Nose © Alan Smith

STAGE 5 Nantwich to Hough 6.9 miles

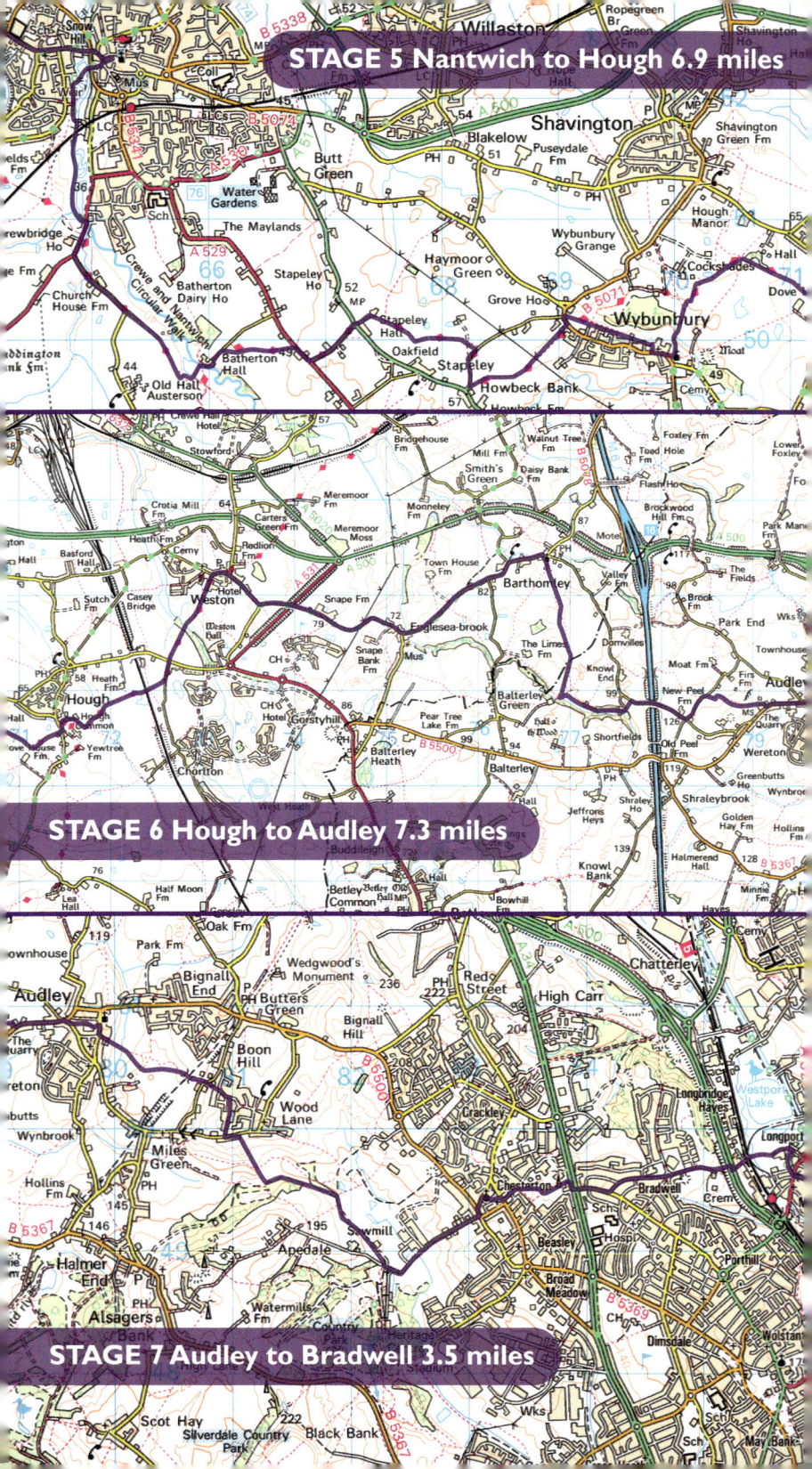

STAGE 6 Hough to Audley 7.3 miles

STAGE 7 Audley to Bradwell 3.5 miles

STAGE 8 Bradwell to Stoke Minster 7.8 miles

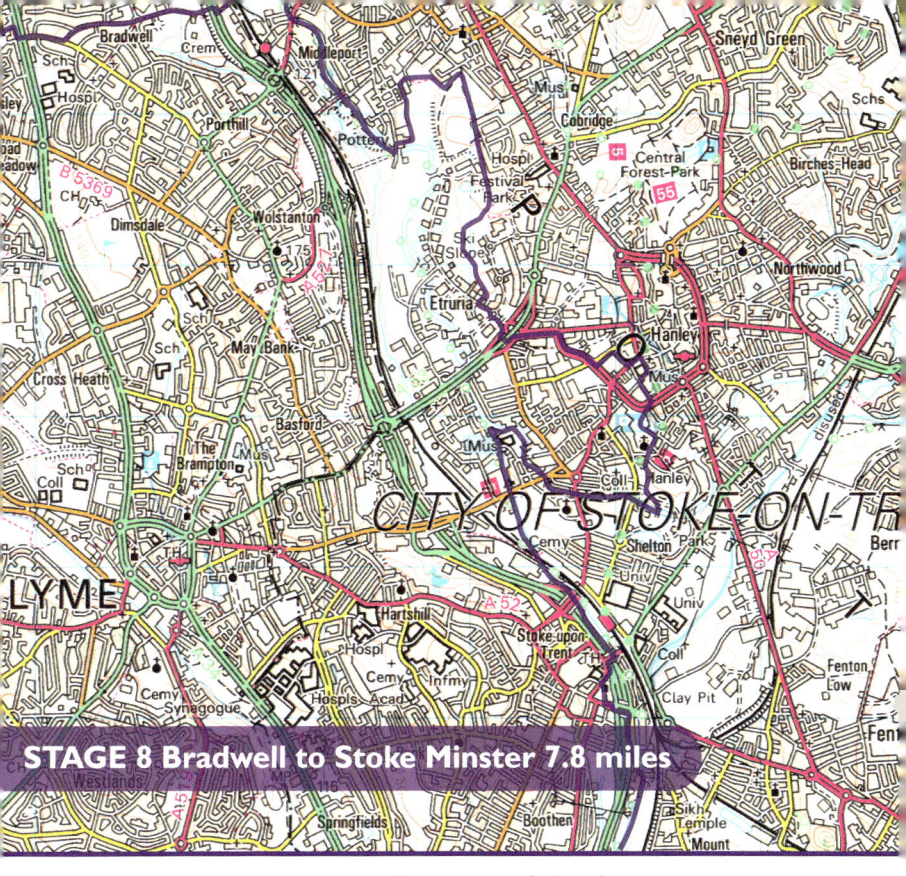

EXPLANATION OF SIGNS

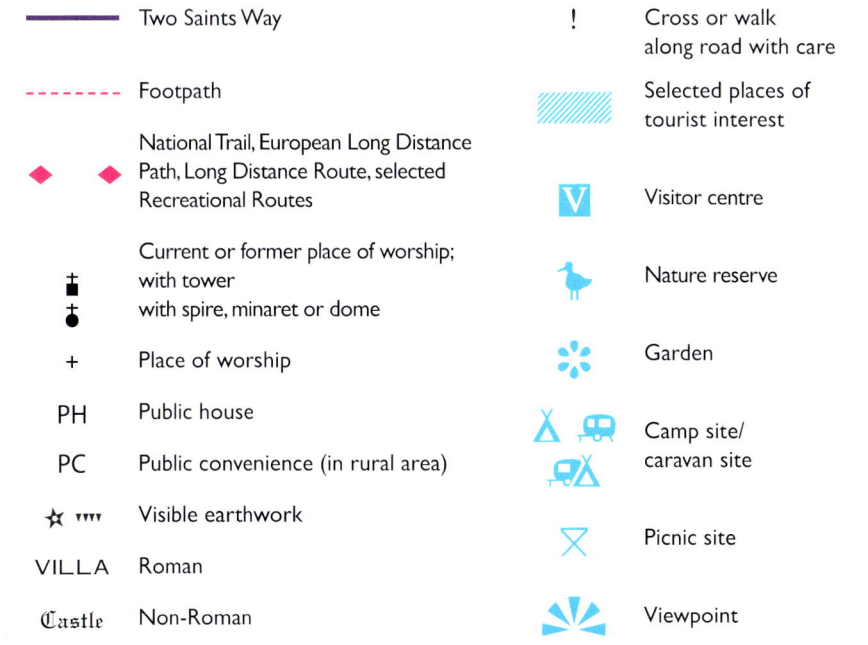

——	Two Saints Way	!	Cross or walk along road with care
-------	Footpath		Selected places of tourist interest
♦ ♦	National Trail, European Long Distance Path, Long Distance Route, selected Recreational Routes	V	Visitor centre
✝ (tower) ✝ (spire)	Current or former place of worship; with tower / with spire, minaret or dome		Nature reserve
+	Place of worship		Garden
PH	Public house		Camp site/ caravan site
PC	Public convenience (in rural area)		
☆ ▼▼▼	Visible earthwork		Picnic site
VILLA	Roman		Viewpoint
Castle	Non-Roman		

SECTION 2 Nantwich to Stoke 25.5 miles

When you leave the church, return the few yards to the pedestrianised High Street and turn left. On your left, you will find the Queen's Aid House. This was built after the Great Fire of 1583 which lasted for 20 days and destroyed most of the town. There is a plaque commemorating the gratitude of the town to Queen Elizabeth I for her help in raising funds to rebuild the town. Take the next road on your right, Mill Street, and then cross straight over Water Lode and the Mill Bridge into the park. Turn immediately left, keeping the River Weaver on your left. After 400 yards cross over to the other side and continue south under the railway bridge. Walk on with the river on your right, and the park and lakes on your left, until you come out at Shrewbridge Road (A530) where you turn right. Cross over the bridge and then take the first left turn into Coole Lane.

For a while you will now follow the Crewe and Nantwich Circular Walk.

Pass Church House Farm and when the road turns right you keep straight on through the kissing gate to the right of the entrance to the Willows.

Go along the track, passing stabling on your right, and soon after by a caravan park, cross over the stile on your right and go half right across the field to the next stile. Cross straight over the field. Continue over into the next field keeping to the right-hand edge. There is a pleasant view of the valley below where you will soon be going. After crossing the next stile, the official right of way goes ahead to the next field boundary and then doubles back to the bridge below, but the landowner is happy to allow walkers to go straight down to the bridge and across a small field to cross another bridge to Batherton. Here the path turns to the right and left round the buildings. About 350 yards after the hall, look out for the footpath sign on your right. Cross over the stile and head for the opposite corner. Cross the stile and then cross another stile into the next field which you cross diagonally, passing a pond with trees on your left. Go over the next stile and head for the corner ahead where you again cross two stiles to reach the A529 and turn right.

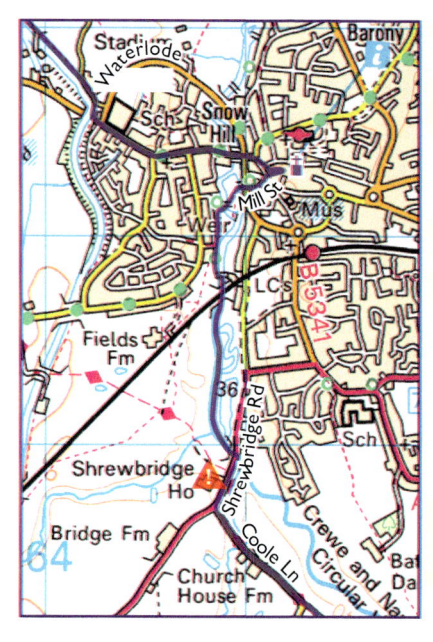

You soon take the next road on your left called First Dig Lane. Go to the end of this road till you reach the A51. Cross straight over into the road opposite leading to Stapeley Hall. Just before the entrance, cross a stile on your right.

STAGE 5 Nantwich to Hough 6.9 miles

Bridge near Batherton © Candice Smith

Passing some farm machinery, go over the next stile and continue over stiles across three fields before you turn left. Keep on the left hand side until you come to an old tree stump which you pass beside and turn to the right. You will see a stile ahead of you. Head for the stile then cross over a road to Yew Tree Farm which is to your left here and on over a couple of stiles over a ditch to join a tarmac road. Turn right here and after 300 yards, take the path to the left and keep the dyke to the left as you cross a field with a number of small ponds. Cross a stile by a gate and turn left down an attractive shady lane. This leads to the village of Wybunbury (pronounced Winbury). Turn left onto the road here and after 80 yards turn right. Cross over the field and two more stiles to reach a lane by a board welcoming you to the Wybunbury Moss National Nature Reserve. Here the Crewe and Nantwich Circular goes left, but you continue straight ahead with a fence on your left and houses on your right. After about 400 yards, pass through a gate. The shaded path leads to the circular driveway for a house on the left. The path goes straight across the driveway. Continue, with evergreens on the right and cross over two more stiles until you come to a stile beside a gate where you turn right into the village down Kiln Lane. Turn left and you will see the tower of the original St Chad's Church ahead of you.

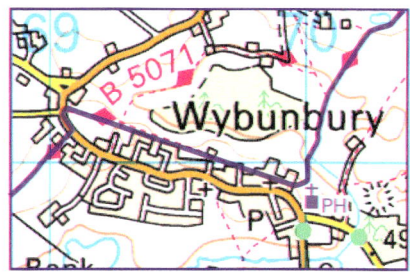

SECTION 2 Nantwich to Stoke 25.5 miles

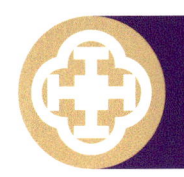

St Chad's Tower

The tower is sometimes called the 'Leaning Tower of South Cheshire' or the 'Hanging Steeple of Wimberie'. This place has been an important Christian centre since Saxon times and the first church was built in the 7th century. The tower was part of a late 15th-century church which was demolished in 1833. The ground here is unstable and later churches, replacing the 15th-century building, were also demolished in 1892 and 1977. The tower itself was stabilised by James Trubshaw in 1832 using a process of underexcavation which was the earliest known use of the technique, a technique later used to stabilise the Leaning Tower of Pisa.

The remains of two medieval moated houses can be seen in fields near to the church. These were 'safe houses' for visiting clergy from Lichfield.

Wybunbury Tower © David Pott

Wybunbury Angry Bishop © Graham Dodd

STAGE 5 Nantwich to Hough 6.9 miles

Wybunbury Moss © John Steadman

Take the footpath down to the left of the church where there is a pleasant view with Wybunbury Moss National Nature Reserve to the left. Cross over the eastern end of it, but if you have time, you might like to explore the reserve and return here. This is a very special wildlife area.

The Moss lies within a hollow left at the end of the last ice age, but salt subsidence has since played a part. Rare plants that live in this unusual, but dangerous mossland habitat include sundew, bog asphodel and bog rosemary. During the summer, look out for colourful dragonflies hunting along the pathways.

After crossing the eastern side of the reserve, start up the hill but do not go up the wide track. Look for the stile to the right which will lead you diagonally across some paddocks and then out by a large pond on your left.

By now you have rejoined the Crewe & Nantwich Circular Walk again. Ahead of you is a large field which you cross over to a kissing gate by a wood on the opposite side. Turn right before that gate and go through the next kissing gate. Keep on the footpath through more kissing gates near the left hand field boundaries until you reach Dove House Farm where you turn left and go through another kissing gate into a rather damp meadow.

Cross over two more stiles to reach the road at Hough where you turn left.

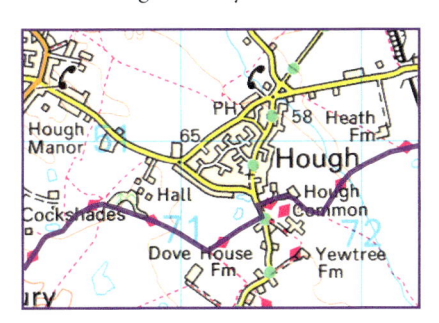

49

SECTION 2 Nantwich to Stoke 25.5 miles

Turn right after passing the football field. The path forks right with the woodland on your right before some houses. Proceed through a kissing gate down the lane with fencing on your left and holly bushes on your right. When you reach the large field you will notice it has some well-spaced oak trees.

Head north-east to the one down to the left. As you approach the tree, keep it to your right and a tree-fringed pond to your left; the stile is ahead of you. Find your way through reedy willow woodland crossing two bridges before crossing a stile into a field. Keep the hedge on your right. Two more stiles lead you over a farm track and across two fields which can be very muddy but there are some helpful duck boards where it is most wet. The path keeps to the left of the hedges, but there is a permissive path on the other side of the hedge that might prove a drier alternative. As you continue, there are ponds in the field to your right. Cross over the railway and take the path which continues straight ahead past stables and over stiles before reaching a road to the right of a Methodist chapel.

Turn left at the chapel into Chorlton Lane. You will soon come to another road which you cross straight over into the field opposite. Walk across the field and then through a wood and over another field, just touching another little piece of woodland on your left before crossing another field. When you get to the next stile take the path to your right to a kissing gate and into a side street (East Avenue) in the village of Weston which you have now reached. Turn right at the main road – Cemetery Road. At the road junction you will come to a small church and the White Lion pub on your right. Turn right here along Main Road. After a third of a mile, turn left on the road to Englesea Brook, crossing over the A531 and passing Snape Farm. A hill before Englesea Brook is something of a novelty! When you reach the village turn right. On your left you will soon arrive at a rather unusual museum devoted to the History of the Primitive Methodists.

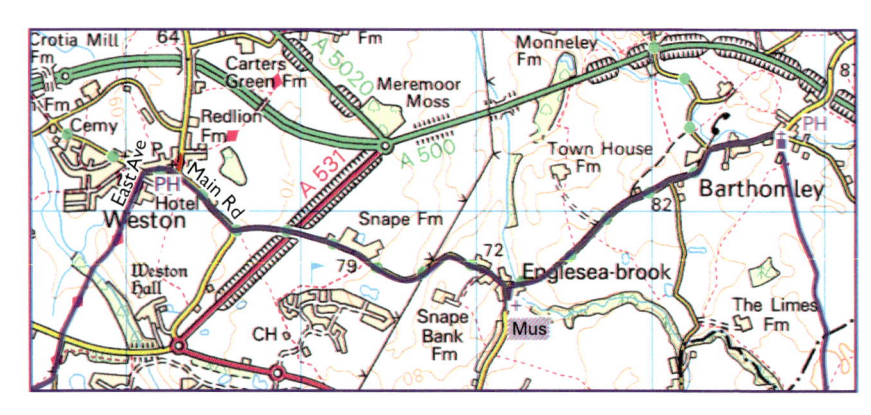

STAGE 6 Hough to Audley 7.3 miles

Englesea Brook Chapel and Museum

The beginnings of the Primitive Methodist movement are usually traced to a remarkable open-air camp meeting that took place in 1807 on Mow Cop, a prominent hill about five miles north-east of here. A distinctive feature of this meeting and others which soon followed was that anyone, including women, could contribute, which was radical at that time. The Primitive Methodists were disparagingly called 'The Ranters'. Those who were the leaders of this initiative had been profoundly influenced by an extraordinary American evangelist called Lorenzo 'Crazy' Dow who visited England on a number of occasions. The revival known as the Second Great Awakening had begun a few years earlier in the USA and fervent camp meetings had been an important feature. Coming in the wake of the French Revolution and amid great nervousness about any radical ideas, the group were expelled from the Methodist church and the Primitive Methodist movement began. It was a mostly working class movement and it made an important contribution to the advent of Trade Unionism.

One of the pioneers of Primitive Methodism, Hugh Bourne, is buried in the cemetery opposite the museum. His prominent tomb is at the end of the lane.

In the museum, the interesting story of this first religious movement in Britain to be influenced from the USA is told by means of a traditional magic lantern show and through a varied collection of artefacts including their banners and musical instruments.

SECTION 2 Nantwich to Stoke 25.5 miles

From the chapel, go back 130 yards north the way you have come and turn right along the road to Barthomley. After a mile, as you approach the village, you will pass a fine timber-framed house, Old Hall Farm, on your left. Continue until you reach the Church of St Bertoline's on your right. The bank on which it stands is a riot of daffodils in spring. The footpath goes right here past the west end of the church, but you may wish to continue a few yards further to enjoy the thatched and timber-framed buildings, including the White Lion Inn, which was built in 1614 and is arguably one of the finest pubs in the country. You should also definitely visit the church which is one of the highlights on the journey.

St Bertoline's Church

Apart from a recent dedication in Stafford, this is the only church dedicated to St Bertoline. We know very little about him, but he is said to have performed a miracle here where a timber Saxon church was probably built. St Bertoline was active in Mercia in the 8th century and is particularly associated with Stafford. He died in the Derbyshire village of Eyam, later famous as the plague village.

A church was built by the Normans in 1090, but little evidence remains apart from a doorway with the characteristic rounded arch which is built into the north wall. The substance of the present church was built of red sandstone in the Perpendicular style during the 15th and 16th centuries with various additions and modifications taking place, including a major restoration in 1852. There are many striking features including the fine carved oak roof, the tombs in the Crewe Chapel, and a charming Tudor altar featuring two panels illustrating the Nativity and the Flight into Egypt. The figures are wearing Tudor hats.

On Christmas Eve in 1643 during the Civil War, the church was the scene of a massacre. Twenty Parliamentarians had taken refuge in the church from Royalist forces, but although they had surrendered twelve of them were murdered.

www.barthomleystbertolines.org.uk

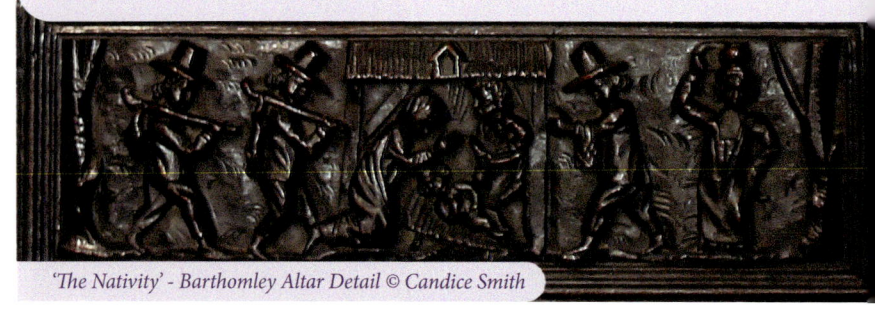

'The Nativity' - Barthomley Altar Detail © Candice Smith

STAGE 6 Hough to Audley 7.3 miles

After you have visited the church, continue past the village hall and a small pond on your left to find a stile into the field on your right. Cross over the stile, turn left and immediately cross another stile and go straight ahead. You will soon see a pond ahead of you – take a line to the right of it up rising ground. As you come towards the field boundary look for the stile about 50 yards to the right of a gate. *(NB Some of the field boundaries marked on the OS Explorer map in this area no longer exist.)* As you cross over the next field, your direction for the next stile is slightly to the right of a tall slender lone tree on the field boundary. Cross over this stile and head down to the field corner ahead and into the next field, keeping the hedge on your left. There are steps up to the next stile. Cross over it and bear right (due south) keeping slightly to the right of higher ground. The route across this field is a permissive path. As you come towards Dean Brook you will see a dead tree ahead of you. Go to the right of it to the boundary hedge and you should find the rather concealed stile for the path which leads down to the valley.

Turn sharp left when you reach the bottom and walk ahead with a pond on your right. *The next half mile along Mill Dale is arguably one of the prettiest stretches on the Two Saints Way.* The steep banks are well endowed with flowers in spring and the valley floor is varied with small fields, dams and bridges. The path keeps on the north bank and passes a house up to your left before coming out onto a gravel road.

Mill Dale © David Pott

Proceed ahead, passing through a gateway and where the gravel driveway bears left at some houses, continue straight ahead on a path which leads up out of the dale. Cross a field and then turn right on the minor road which soon leads you across the M6.

At the next crossroads by New Peel Farm, turn left into Moat Lane. After 200 yards, the road bears right and soon after, take the footpath on your right and go up Kent Hill through kissing gates while keeping to the right-hand field boundary. There is an underground reservoir to your right. On a good day there are fine views from here. Behind you is the Cheshire Plain with the Welsh hills in the distance. Mow Cop, with its folly, is to the north-east. After you have made your way through more kissing gates with railings to your left, good views of Audley open up with the Wedgwood Monument prominent on the hill behind it. Go down the hill and along a lane to reach the road which you cross over and turn left to head into Audley. After a quarter of a mile take the first road on your right (Chester Road) and then look for the shady footpath on your left which leads you up to a road with St James' Church on the opposite side.

SECTION 2 Nantwich to Stoke 25.5 miles

Walk south downhill from the church and take the next road on your left (Hall Street) and pass Audley Theatre on your left. Ahead of you are attractive railings and the way into Leddy's Field Wildlife area.

Go down the steps into the reserve and continue down and cross a bridge with a pond to the left. Go on ahead through the kissing gate and the path goes straight up hill with a hedge on the left. At the field boundary, cross a duck board and go through the hedge gap and fork right and initially walk 50 yards towards a prominent tree, then turn left by the fence, passing another tree on your left. Go downhill and across a damp patch to cross a stile and then go down a lane which can be muddy at times. This opens out into a field. After 60 yards turn right into the next field. The path goes straight ahead but you may choose to skirt around this damp section before finding the next stile across a small field leading to a path across the disused railway. Enter a paddock and head across stiles to a narrow hedge-lined path which leads to a road.

Turn left then right up a path known as 'Narrow Nick', which is flanked by holly bushes either side and which leads into the residential area of Boon Hill. Turn right here into Birch Road. After passing two roads on your right, you will find the next footpath on your right. Pass a field and children's play area on your left and this leads into a road which soon reaches a T-junction. Turn left here and shortly after passing Wood Lane Primary School, turn right towards Riley's Field play area. **Fork left down the footpath into the woods. You are now in Apedale Country Park.**

Apedale Community Country Park

Apedale consists of 154 hectares of woodland, wetland and grassland, managed by Staffordshire County Council, and home to a diverse range of flora and fauna, including brown hare, grass snake, lapwing and great crested newt. This area was once rich in deposits of coal, iron ore and clay, making it a hive of industrial activity, evidence of which may still be seen. Today, there are walking, cycling and horse routes, a heritage museum and railway, and a new visitor centre, built and powered using the latest green technology.

Continue ahead at the bottom of the valley and over an open area frequented by bikers at the weekend. When you come to the next T-junction turn left along the track which was formerly a disused railway. After half a mile you pass a green barrier. Burley Farm on your right and Thorp Precast (marked as a sawmill on some maps) on your left are the next landmarks. The footpath leads to another metal barrier. Ahead are some narrow gauge railway tracks in

STAGE 7 Audley to Bradwell 3.5 miles

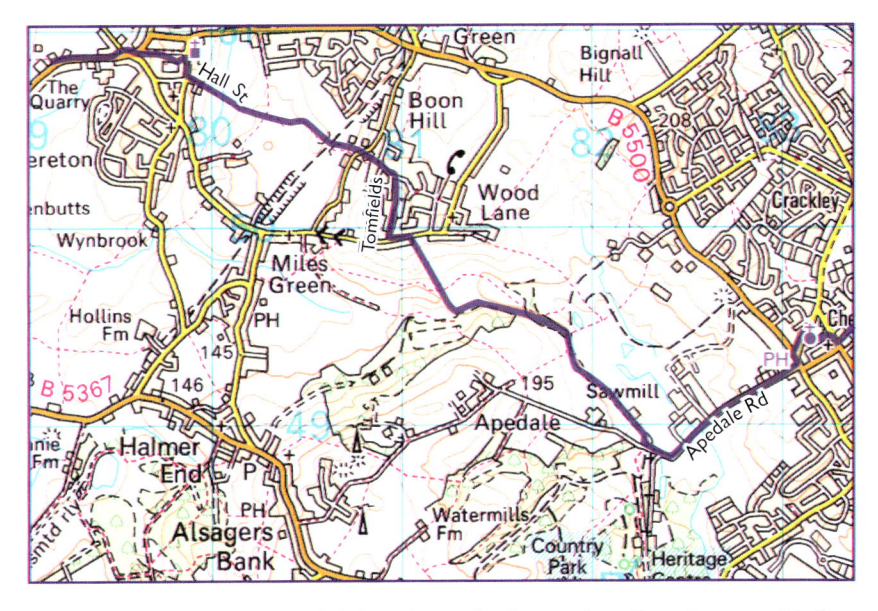

Apedale Country Park. Turn left here down the dirt track. Follow this round left, passing works on the left and up Apedale Road to Chesterton. Turn left at the top of Apedale Road, cross the road and then take the first right into Church Street, past the Red Lion Pub on your right – Holy Trinity Church is nearby.

Chesterton

In Roman times there was an auxiliary fort here and also a thriving Romano-British township.

At Holy Trinity Church there is a significant stone from Anglo-Saxon times which features a relief carving thought to be of St Michael. It was found in a field and had been used as feeding trough for cattle!

In much more recent times, Chesterton was a mining village. The colliery closed in 1988.

Chesterton Saxon Stone © Candice Smith

SECTION 2 Nantwich to Stoke 25.5 miles

From Holy Trinity Church, walk down the tarmac path across the green. Cross over the road to the shops and turn right, then left up Brick Kiln Lane. You will see the Salvation Army Hall ahead of you. Keep that on your left and the wooden fencing on your right and then take the footpath on your right. As you rise up to the mast another path crosses. Don't join it but head up the bank until you reach the top. Then turn left along the path past the mast. In winter and spring there are good views here over The Potteries.

The Potteries

The history of the area is closely connected to the ceramics industry which was certainly in existence by the 12th century. An entry in the [Staffordshire] Pipe Roll records the purchase and despatch of 4000 plates and 500 cups for the King's Christmas feast held at Tewskbury in 1204 (Oxford History of England, vol. 3, p. 84 1951). Plentiful supplies of clay, as well as salt and lead for glazing and coal to fire the kilns, made it ideal for making pottery. The renowned Josiah Wedgwood set up his business in 1759 and in the following years the industry was transformed during the Industrial Revolution from a cottage-based to a factory-based industry. One of Britain's first large factories was built by Wedgwood's at Etruria in 1769.

The brilliance and technical innovation of Wedgwood and other famous families like the Spodes, Woods and Copelands ensured that the area remained at the forefront of the ceramics industry into the 20th century. A major feature of the landscape was the existence of up to 4,000 bottle kilns.

As the villages of The Potteries became towns, calls for them to be amalgamated became frequent, resulting in the County Borough of Stoke-on-Trent being formed in 1910 comprising Burslem, Hanley, Longton, Stoke, Fenton and Tunstall. It acquired city status in 1925, although it still retains a village/town feel in each of the towns and their many distinct sub-districts. In October 2010 novelist Margaret Drabble, reviewing the book The Lost City of Stoke-on-Trent, said of the city, 'The Potteries are one of the strangest regions in the British Isles.' They can also be one of the friendliest – don't be surprised if people start spontaneously chatting with you on the slightest pretext!

STAGE 7 Audley to Bradwell 3.5 miles

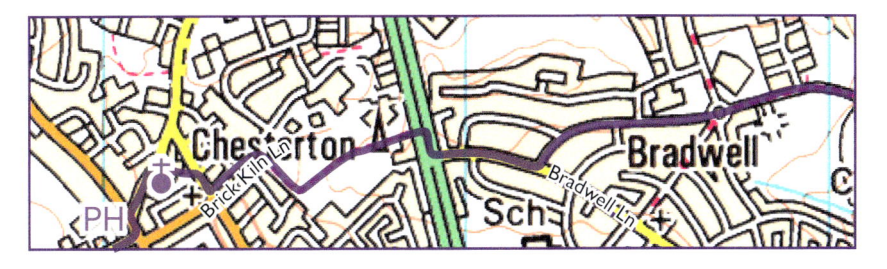

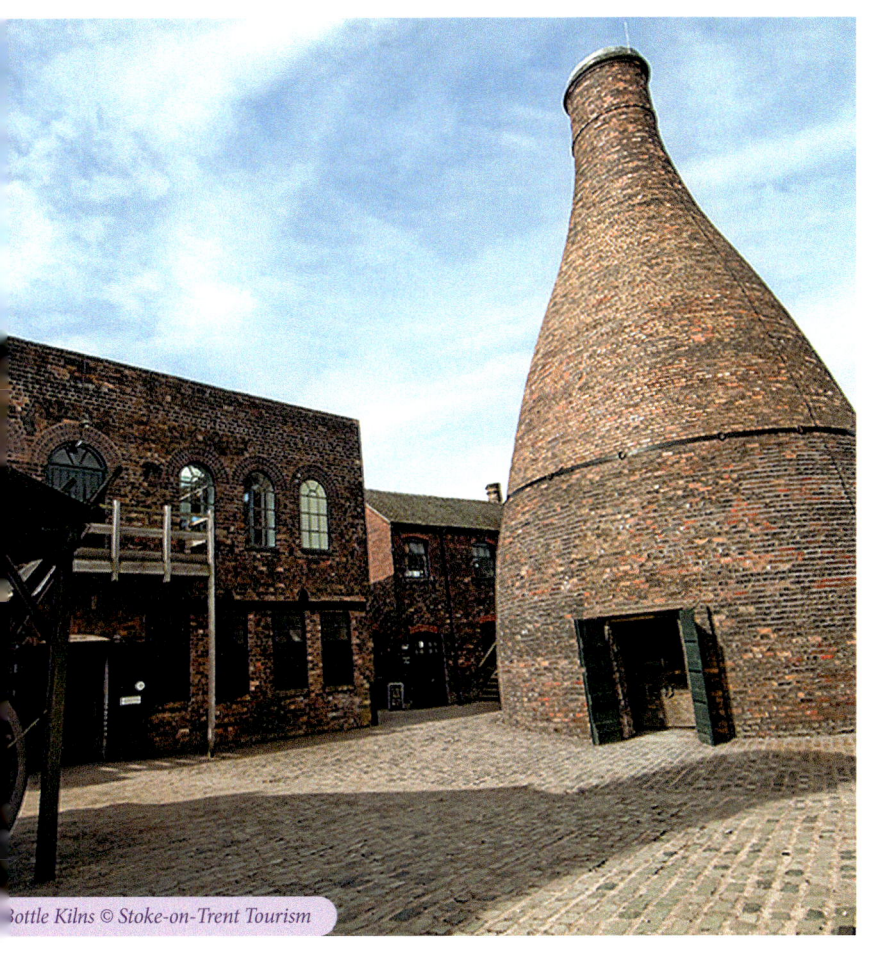

Bottle Kilns © Stoke-on-Trent Tourism

57

SECTION 2 Nantwich to Stoke 25.5 miles

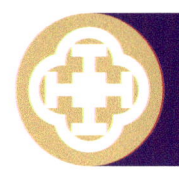

Turn right and then cross over the A34 at the lights into Bradwell Lane. Take the third road on the left – Bursley Way. Eventually you come to a school on your left. Go straight over the roundabout into Chatterley Close. A few yards before the end of the road, take the footpath ahead of you which descends steeply through woods to an underpass at the A500. Turn slightly right and left into Peel Street and then cross the footbridge over the railway. The path goes straight ahead through patchy woodland and past a mill on the right to reach the Trent and Mersey Canal, where you turn right.

This is a significant point on the pilgrimage where the predominantly easterly direction of the route becomes predominantly southerly.

Before you make your right turn you may wish to walk a few yards up the canal to Westport Lake where there is a visitor centre with good facilities and refreshments available.

This area is called Longport and the other ports nearby – Westport, Middleport and Newport indicate that this was where the wharfingering communities, which handled the import and export of cargoes to The Potteries, once existed. There is a fine bottle kiln on the opposite side of the canal before you pass under the busy A527 (bridge no 126).

Continue down the canal and note Middleport Pottery on the opposite side. At the next bridge (no 125), you may well want to cross over and double back the 250 yards to

The Trent & Mersey Canal

The idea of this canal linking the two rivers to provide a water transport link from the east coast to the west coast was that of the great canal builder James Brindley and the potter Josiah Wedgwood. A high percentage of Wedgwood's pottery was broken as it was transported on the rutted turnpike roads and he knew that this canal link would enable the pottery industry in the area to export more efficiently both nationally and globally.

The canal was authorised by Act of Parliament in 1766 and Josiah Wedgwood cut the first sod at Middleport. The whole canal of 93 miles with 70 locks and 5 tunnels was opened only 11 years later. The canal was therefore a key element in the prosperity of The Potteries. There was still heavy traffic on the canal into the 1960s, with cargoes of salt, beer and coal as well as pottery. The canal is now part of the Cheshire and Four Counties cruising rings and sees around 10,000 boats a year plying this stretch.

STAGE 8 Bradwell to Stoke Minster 7.8 miles

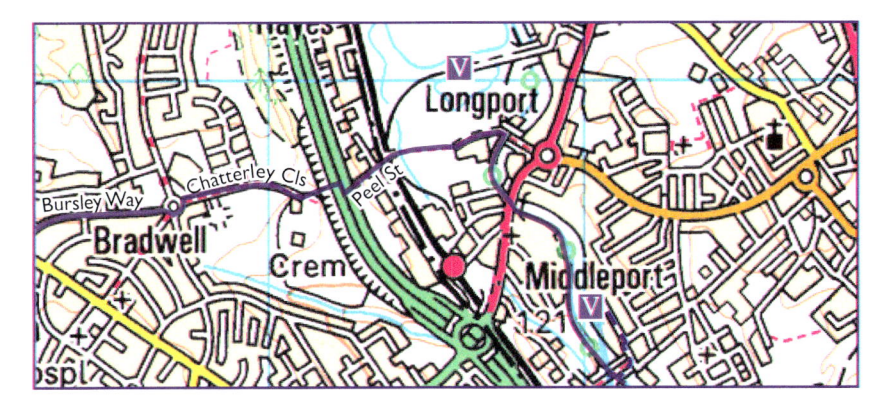

Middleport Pottery which has an excellent visitor centre and café. See **middleportpottery.co.uk**. Walk on along the towpath until you reach bridge no 123. After passing under the bridge, turn right and go over the bridge. On your left is Oliver's Mill built in 1909. It includes two calcining ovens, one in the traditional bottle shape and the other one square with a heavily moulded cap.

To your right is the site of the old Burslem Port. The Burslem Arm was a short stretch of canal into the centre of Burslem. It was built in 1805 but it was closed by a major breach in 1961 into the valley. The Burslem Port Project hopes to restore the canal.

Middleport Pottery © David Haden

SECTION 2 Nantwich to Stoke 25.5 miles

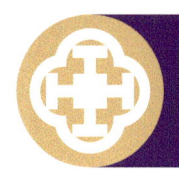

Continue ahead along Newport Lane, then turn right into Luke Street alongside the new development of apartments. At the end of Luke Street turn left behind the apartments on a wide path. At the end of the wide path, turn right to take a narrow path down and over an old canal bridge. Go straight over past another scrap dealers on the right, cross the access track to their entrance and go on into a field ahead of you.

After a few yards, fork slightly right and head for the corner of the houses ahead of you. When you reach them turn right and then left around them with allotments on your right. Turn right at the end of the allotments and on a small grassy track cross over one path and over to another one where you turn right, soon passing a pond on your left. You are now in Grange Park. In medieval times a farm here supplied food for the monks at Hulton Abbey which is now called Abbey Hulton! Continue straight ahead and then up some steps. Turn right passing a playground on your right and houses on your left. Walk on, soon passing the Grange Park Greenway sign and then a cricket ground on your left.

You are now entering Festival Park where the National Garden Festival was held in 1986. It is an intriguing area where various objects left over from the festival can still be discovered. When the tarmac runs out, go ahead across a circular brick structure to pass between some palm trees on a small rise. Continue straight ahead on a path between trees and ascend a bank, keeping the allotments to your left. At the top there is a good view across the retail park to Hanley. Go down the hill towards the tarmac path on the right, aiming for a point about 50 yards short of its junction with another (by a waste bin).

Take the path opposite, passing a low wooden palisade. After a further 130 yards look out to your left for a bridge that crosses a small ravine – all of this fashioned for the festival. After a further 130 yards, look to your left for a bridge that crosses a small ravine. This has now been closed, so walk down to the left and then up the opposite bank to rejoin the path. You will then pass a standing stone on your right.

Go across and straight on to the fence ahead, then turn left. Fork left to pass some eucalyptus trees on your right and then go half right passing another stand of eucalyptus in a wood and stone circle – this time on your left. Fork right and continue, passing two sets of steps on your right. When you come out onto a wider path turn right and ahead you will

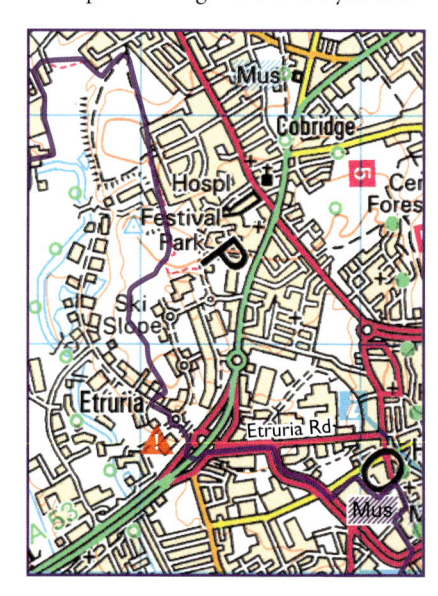

60

STAGE 8 Bradwell to Stoke Minster 7.8 miles

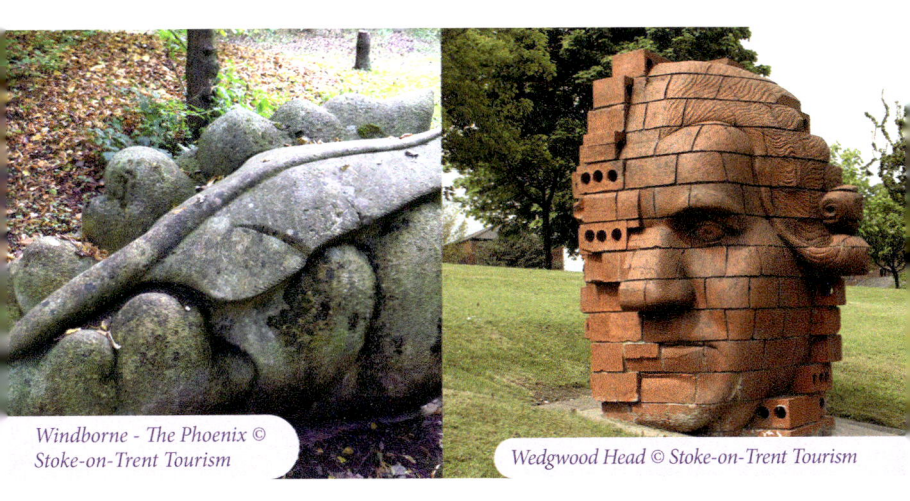

Windborne - The Phoenix © Stoke-on-Trent Tourism

Wedgwood Head © Stoke-on-Trent Tourism

find a stone circle. Turn left here and go down the straight path. You will pass a sculpture on your left called 'Windborne – the Phoenix' by Keir Smith. After this the path rises to a final circular grass patch. Go to the right of it and on the far side descend flights of steps, then keep turning right as you go down. You will come to a Welsh slate path which steepens where there was once a waterfall.

The path comes out opposite the Moat House Hotel. Cross the road here and turn left. The building on the left of the Moat House Hotel complex – set back on your right across the grass – is the Etruria Hall where Josiah Wedgwood once lived. Next on your right you will pass a colossal head of Josiah Wedgwood made from large bricks.

At the roundabout with a swan sculpture in the middle, cross over Marina Way and continue ahead, keeping the Odeon Cinema on your right. As you head for the pedestrian lights to take you to the A53, look out for the J Arthur Rank gong man on what was the entrance sign for the Festival Garden.

The pedestrian lights take you under the A53 flyover. Immediately ahead of you, you will find the entrance to a surprising footpath which was once The Potteries Loop Line. Many people use this, but strictly speaking it is not a Public Right of Way so turn left and then right into Etruria Road. After a quarter of a mile turn right into Potteries Way in front of the new Premier Inn. Cross over at the next lights, continue to Tesco's and turn left to walk along the front of it. Curiously this is the only shop that is directly on your route between Chesterton and Tittensor! Turn right, keeping Tesco's on your right until you reach Broad Street where you turn left.

The Potteries Museum is on the other side of the road so cross over at the lights to reach the entrance in Bethesda Street.

SECTION 2 Nantwich to Stoke 25.5 miles

The Potteries Museum & Art Gallery and the Staffordshire Hoard

The Potteries Museum is the highlight of Hanley's Cultural Quarter. It houses the world's largest collection of Staffordshire ceramics and also contains galleries dedicated to local and natural history, costume and paintings. There is also a Supermarine Spitfire from World War II on permanent display.

Since February 2010, The Potteries Museum & Art Gallery has been the home of a number of artefacts from the Staffordshire Hoard. The Staffordshire Hoard was originally unearthed in a field near Lichfield by metal detector enthusiast Terry Herbert in July 2009. Almost 4,000 pieces were recovered, predominantly of gold and silver. The objects have been dated between the late 6th and early 8th centuries and were valued at £3.3 million. It is arguably the most significant archaeological find from the Anglo-Saxon period and is changing our perceptions of the ancient kingdom of Mercia.

Stoke Museums along with Birmingham Museum have purchased the Hoard, and at the Potteries Museum the Hoard is the centrepiece of the Anglo-Saxon Kingdom of Mercia exhibition.

On leaving the main entrance to the museum, turn right. There is a small park on your right which you cross diagonally to reach Warner Street. Go ahead to reach Potteries Way again and turn right. The building on your right here with the bottle oven was formerly Smithfield Pottery. Cross straight over at the pedestrian lights into Hinde Street which soon bears left. You will see the conspicuous City Central Mosque ahead and you turn right at the end of Hinde Street to reach it. You would be welcome to visit. If the mosque is closed, phone Rana M Tufail on 01782 610 548 and he may be available to open up and show you round.

Continue a few yards after the mosque, cross the road and enter Hanley Park which was landscaped by Thomas Mawson and opened in 1897. Pass a playground on your right and keep on the wide path until you see a bandstand. Turn right here down steps and go over the ornamental bridge and join the Caldon Canal turning right (west).

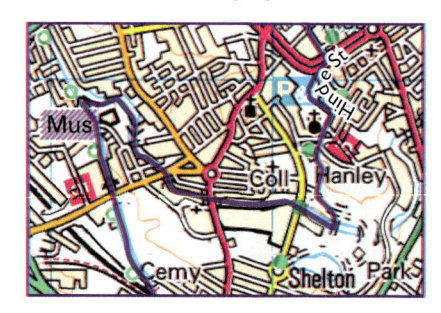

STAGE 8 Bradwell to Stoke Minster 7.8 miles

Saxon Hoard © The Potteries Museum & Art Gallery

The Caldon Canal

This delightful 18-mile canal is a branch of the Trent & Mersey and was completed in 1779. When the Trent & Mersey Canal was nearing completion it was discovered that the water supply to the canal was inadequate so this branch was built to tap into the plentiful water supplies from the Staffordshire Moorlands, while at the same time to carry limestone which was transported to Froghall Wharf from Caldon Low Quarries. It also carried coal from the Cheadle Coalfield and ironstone from the iron ore mines in the Churnet valley. Use of the canal declined in the middle of the 20th century so that by 1960 it was virtually unusable. Between 1970 and 1974 it was restored as part of the UK's first canal restoration projects.

Follow the towpath, passing Planet Lock and the staircase locks at Bedford Street until you reach the Etruria Industrial Museum site where you rejoin the Trent & Mersey Canal. Turn left to resume the journey south.

SECTION 2 Nantwich to Stoke 25.5 miles

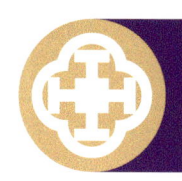

Etruria

Etruria was named after a district in Italy where the Etruscans developed designs which were a major inspiration for the great potter Josiah Wedgwood. He established his works here in 1769 and they remained in operation until 1950 when the factory moved a few miles south to Barlaston.

The Etruria Junction where the Caldon Canal meets the Trent & Mersey Canal is one of the most attractive canalscapes in the country with its intriguing juxtaposition of locks. The Etruria Industrial Museum is home to Jesse Shirley's 1857 Bone and Flint Mill. On occasions the 1903 boiler is fired to power 'Princess' the 1820s beam engine when the machinery can be seeing working. Other features include a statue of James Brindley, the great engineer who started the canal systems, a graving dock and an unusual signpost to Uttoxeter.

Etruria Junction © David Pott

Passing the impressive flight of Stoke Locks, you pass an old flour mill and Hanley Cemetery on the opposite bank. The two bottle ovens on the right are part of the Lock 38 residential development which is sited on the place of the invention of the flushing toilet. A new ideal 'model' factory, Cliffe Vale Pottery, was built here by T. W. Twyford in 1887, and his factory manufactured the world's first flushing toilets and other innovative sanitaryware for over a hundred years, changing the way billions of people lived around the world. The Twyford's works closed in 1994 and moved to a purpose-built factory at Alsager.

You then pass under railway bridges. The next bridge is the A52 and then

STAGE 8 Bradwell to Stoke Minster 7.8 miles

immediately after that is the sloping bridge no. 113. After you have passed under it, turn right up the steps and then go diagonally right up across a road which leads you to the bridge over the A500. **Follow this road (Glebe Street) round to the left to the next significant destination – Stoke Minster.**

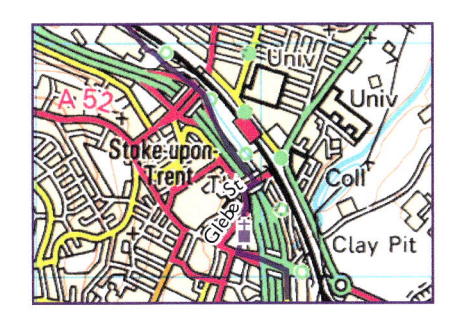

Stoke Minster

This church was designated as Stoke Minster as recently as 2005. This was highly appropriate because it was most probably the earliest place of Christian worship in the area and therefore a mother church in the region. The earliest church would have been built in the 7th or 8th centuries. In the graveyard there is an 8th-century preaching cross with fine knotwork designs – indeed some believe that this is the origin of the Staffordshire Knot. The font from the Saxon church is in the present church. The second church was built in Norman times and two arches from it have been restored and stand in the graveyard. The present church was built from 1826 and consecrated in 1830. The church was formerly known as St Peter ad Vincula (St Peter in chains) before it became a minster. There are ceramic memorials in the church to the great potters of the region and Josiah Wedgwood is buried in the churchyard. There is also a memorial to the legendary footballer Sir Stanley Matthews.

Saxon Cross © Richard Redshaw

STAGE 9 Stoke Minster to Tittensor 6.8 miles

STAGE 10 Tittensor to Stone 4.9 miles

STAGE 11 Stone to Sandon 4.9 miles

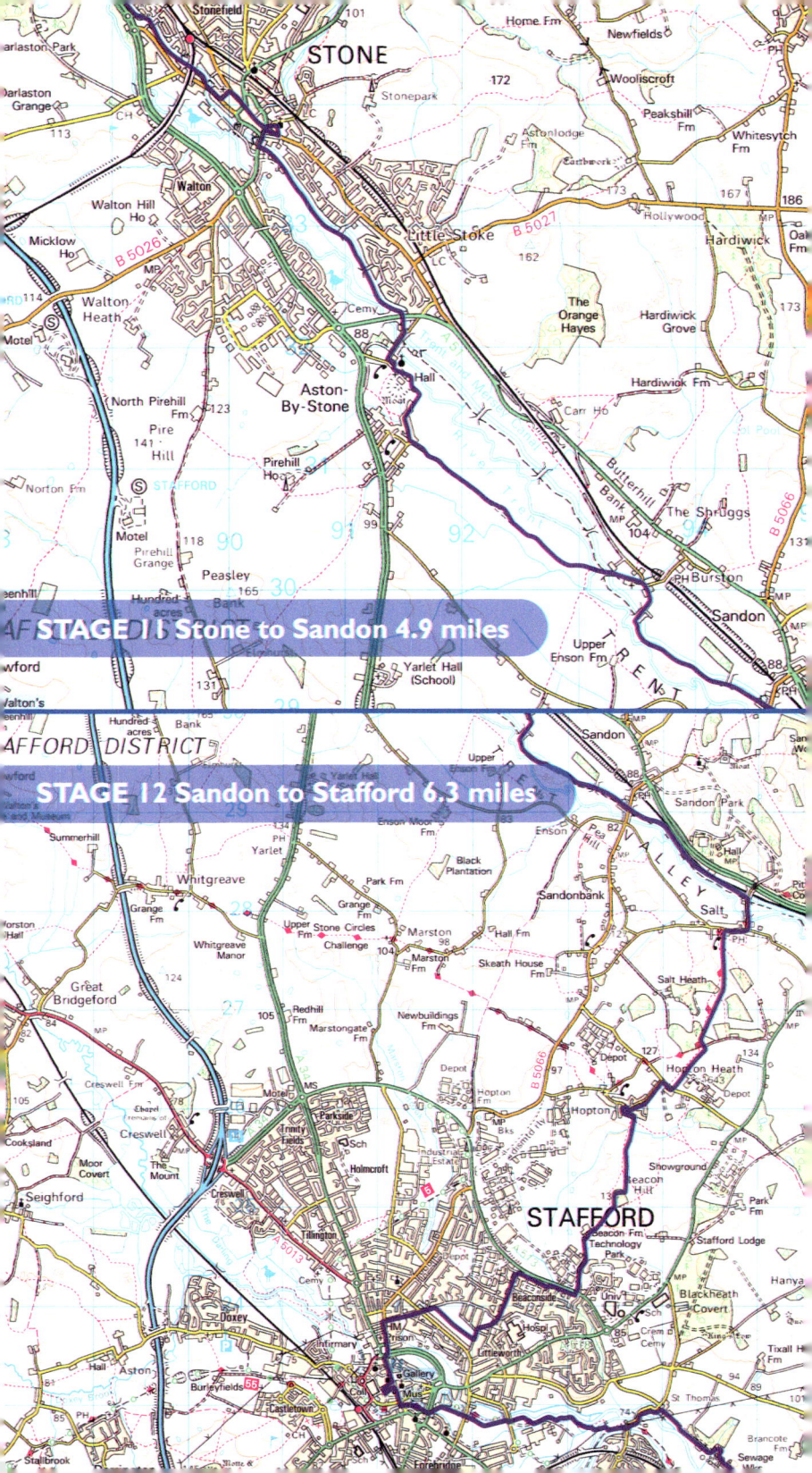

STAGE 12 Sandon to Stafford 6.3 miles

SECTION 3 Stoke to Stafford 23 miles

Stoke Minster Arches © David Pott

From the entrance to Stoke Minster turn left (south) to view the Saxon preaching cross and walk under the 13th century arches (sometimes locally referred to as the MacDonald Arches!) to find the tomb of Josiah Wedgwood. From here, exit the churchyard into Church Street and turn left up to the traffic lights and cross over to the southern side, then cross over the traffic lights at the slip road off the A500 and the way back down to the canal will be on your right. Continue southwards. Where the canal crosses the infant River Trent, you pass a boatyard which curiously also offers fishing, shooting and line dancing! A mile further on you pass under the A50 and the huge incinerator on your right. On the opposite side is the Britannia Stadium, the home of Stoke City Football Club.

Continue onwards for a mile, with the first open countryside for a while on your right. Shortly after the canal bends to the

Trentham Gardens

STAGE 9 Stoke Minster to Tittensor 6.8 miles

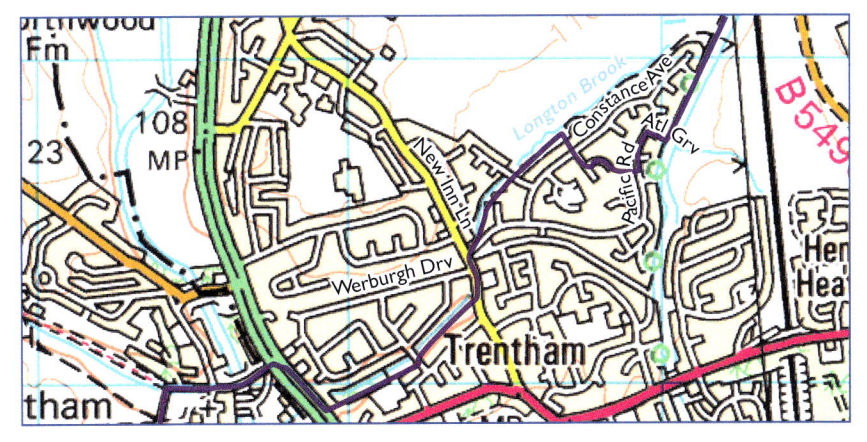

right, you come to a housing estate on your right. Walk a further 350 yards and then go down a ramp into the estate. At the end of the cul-de-sac which is called Atlantic Grove, turn left into Pacific Road. After a further 100 yards, look out for a short connecting footpath located behind a high hedge after no. 119. This leads into Michigan Grove. Turn right into Winnipeg Close. Cross straight over Constance Avenue to the path ahead of you and then left to follow the pleasant Longton Brook for the next mile. It is alive with birdsong and flowers in spring, as well as a powerful aroma of wild garlic. Cross over one road but when you come to the next road (Pacific Road) do not go over to the cycle path opposite but turn right and then left down New Inn Lane. After passing Werburgh Drive on your right, you cross Longton Brook again and turn right to keep following this attractive walk. You cross over another road and continue until you reach the A34.

Trentham Estate and Gardens

Trentham is first recorded as a royal manor in 1086 in the Doomsday Book. For a while it was in the hands of the Earls of Chester before Henry II claimed it in 1153 and created a royal deer park. In 1541, the estate was obtained by a Wolverhampton wool merchant named James Leveson. For 380 years the estate was to be owned by his descendants. The first Trentham Hall was built in the early 17th century and was remodelled several times. The most significant developments, including the establishment of the Italian Gardens, took place under the second Duke of Sutherland in the mid 19th century. In 1996, St Modwen's Properties and the German investor Willi Reitz bought the estate and began the transformation of the site into the prime tourist attraction that it is today.

SECTION 3 Stoke to Stafford 23 miles

Turn right up the A34 and when you come to traffic lights cross over to the old gates to Trentham Hall and take the road to the left just before the Harvester. Cross the bridge over the River Trent and turn left. After passing a courtyard, you will arrive at St Mary's Trentham also on your left.

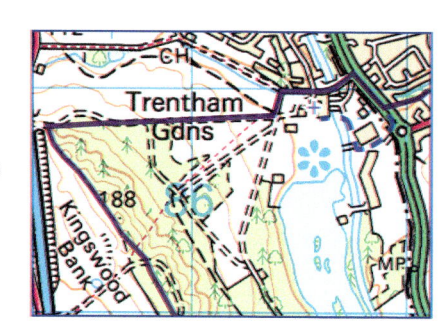

Alternative route

When you reach the A34, you may prefer to divert to all the facilities at the Trentham Estate in which case turn left and cross over at the lights. To rejoin the Two Saints Way, pass in front of the garden centre and then turn right following the River Trent and then crossing it before going through a courtyard. Turn left to find St Mary's Church, Trentham.

St Mary's Church, Trentham

There has been a place of worship here since the 7th century and some believe that St Werbergh was the first abbess of a nunnery here. In the churchyard is the base of a Saxon cross which features a praying stone. The stone below it has been worn by the knees of supplicants over the centuries. If you would like to follow them, you may wish to fill out a prayer request form which can be found to the left of the gateway as you enter the churchyard.

In the mid 12th century a priory was built here by Hugh Lupus, Earl of Chester. The present church was built by the second Duke of Sutherland in 1844, but the architect Sir Charles Barry incorporated Norman pillars and other old stonework from the former church as well as the fine Jacobean rood screen. The tiled floor was a gift from Herbert Minton. From the south door there is a spectacular view of the Italian Gardens and the lake.

STAGE 9 Stoke Minster to Tittensor 6.8 miles

After visiting St Mary's, do not turn immediately left, but return to Park Drive and turn left. After 100 yards, turn left over a bridge, go through the kissing gate and straight ahead. As you approach a high fence, fork right on to a wide track heading towards a wooden gate. You are now on a straight attractive path through the woods. This was once a main drive to Trentham Hall. After passing by a second wooden gate you will come to the M6. Just before it, turn steeply up to the left. This path leads you up to an area known as Seven Sisters. Some suppose this is because you may count seven hillocks along the ridge, but it was more likely named after a stand of beech trees. Between the path and the M6 below is an attractive heathland area which is a rare and threatened habitat in the Midlands.

The new woodland to the east is one of just sixty Diamond Woods which was created in partnership with the Woodland Trust to celebrate Queen Elizabeth's Diamond Jubilee in 2012. The wood contains almost 10,000 Sessile Oak which should thrive in the shallow soil of this area which once supplied the gravels in support of the construction of the M6 motorway close by. Rare breed Red Poll cattle have recently been introduced to support the conservation grazing of the grass land within the parkland and also the heath.

Pilgrim at the praying stone at St Mary's Trentham © Tim Saxton

SECTION 3 Stoke to Stafford 23 miles

King's Wood © Candice Smith

Black Fallow Deer © Graham Walker

Keeping on the main path near the top of the ridge, go through a gateway to enter into King's Wood. To your right are fields leading down to a lake and the M6 motorway. You may prefer a narrower parallel path 10 to 15 yards to your left which is also drier after wet weather. Keep a lookout for the black fallow deer which are frequently seen here. After two-thirds of a mile, the path goes steeply down to a stream and then steeply up again. The high fence of the Trentham Monkey Forest is on your left. Some of the Barbary macaques that live here roost overnight at this end, so you are unlikely to see them unless you pass by early morning or late evening.

As you leave the Monkey Forest, keep a fence on your right as you walk uphill. Pause at the top to enjoy the view to the east across the Trent Valley. Barlaston Hall is directly opposite. It was built in 1756 and eventually bought by the most famous pottery family – the Wedgwoods. Below to the left is the Wedgwood Visitor Centre and factory. The wooded hill to the south-east is crowned by the huge statue of the Duke of Sutherland which is your next destination. Where the wider path swings down to the left, continue ahead to go through a gate and into the wood. Go along the path keeping on higher ground. After about 400 yards, you will come to a gate and stile and ahead of you is the monument with its commanding views. Trentham Lake is in the foreground with the Italian Gardens at the far end and Stoke spreads back into the valleys and hills beyond. Mow Cop with its folly is due north and to the north-east is the Peak District.

STAGE 9 Stoke Minster to Tittensor 6.8 miles

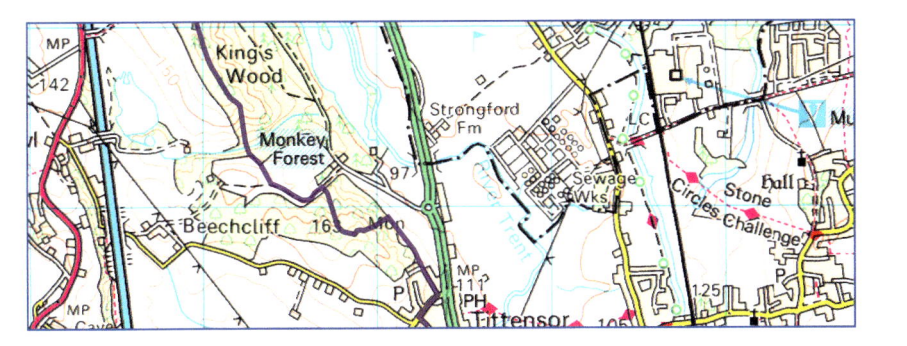

The Duke of Sutherland Monument

This colossal statue of the first Duke of Sutherland was designed by Charles Winks and sculptured by Sir Francis Leggatt Chantrey.

The first Duke's family name was Leveson-Gower and Trentham Hall was their ancestral home. His wife-to-be, Countess Elizabeth, was the daughter of the 18th Earl of Sutherland, a completely separate family, whose possessions included Dunrobin Castle and the entire County of Sutherland. In 1771, at the age of seven, Elizabeth applied to the House of Lords for her late father's title; this application was granted and she became known as Countess Elizabeth of Sutherland and Baroness Strathnaver. In 1785, Countess Elizabeth, who was Britain's greatest heiress, married George Granville Leveson-Gower. Some 48 years later he was made a Duke in recognition of his political service and, as a compliment to his wife, chose as his title the name Sutherland. He is estimated to have been the wealthiest man in Britain in the 19th century.

The weather-worn inscription gives some indication of the Duke's local popularity. While he achieved much in Staffordshire itself he became better known in relation to the Highland Clearances. Thousands of families were forcibly evicted and their homes burnt to make way for sheep. They were then resettled along the coast or in Canada. It is widely held that his actions led to destruction of the Highland way of life.

Take the footpath directly behind the monument and fork left. When you reach a dip in the ground ahead turn left and descend through the woods on a spur off the hill to reach a gate out of the woods where you turn right and very soon pass through a gate and walk down Monument Lane with its attractive cottages on the left. You are now in the village of Tittensor.

SECTION 3 Stoke to Stafford 23 miles

From Monument Lane, turn right up Winghouse Lane, then left past the post office and village store and continue along Copeland Avenue. You come to St Luke's Tittensor which is usually open.

Tittensor

St Luke's Tittensor © David Pott

This is the only place of this name in the world. In the Domesday Book of 1086 it is called Titesovere. Titten derives from an old English name Titta and the meaning which is appropriate to the local geography is 'Titta's slope'. A manor house belonging to the de Tittensor family once existed here and a number of descendants of that original Tittensor family still live locally. The manor house was demolished in 1834. Some of the materials were used to build St Luke's Church in 1880, including the carved wooden panelling in the chancel. The timber-framed clock tower is a particularly attractive feature of the church.

Return to the street, turning left down Bracken Close. At the T-junction, look across to your right for the footpath sign between houses and into woodland where you turn right. The path soon descends to cross below the lower end of a small reservoir. Turn right along a pleasant track with the reservoir and a smaller pond on your right. When you come to the gate, turn left up the road. Before you do this, you may like to go and have a look at the rich variety of ornamental ducks on the lake a few yards to your right on Beechdale Road.

74

STAGE 10 Tittensor to Stone 4.9 miles

Saxon's Lowe © David Pott

Nuns Walk © David Pott

Continue up the road passing Groundslow Farm on your right and pass a wood (Cumberstone Wood) on your left. At the end of it turn immediately left up the path, keeping the wood on your left. Cross straight over a road and go ahead to Tittensor Chase. To your left there is pleasant parkland belonging to the Copeland family who made their money in the pottery industry. At one point there is a good view across the Trent Valley to Barlaston Hall. There has been significant storm damage in this area.

Before you leave Tittensor Chase, you will notice on your left a prominent mound. This is called Saxon's Lowe. This mound possibly dates from the Iron Age period. In which case why is it called Saxon's Lowe? One possibility is that because it already had associations as a significant burial place, it was chosen by King Wulphere, the Saxon King of Mercia as his special place of burial. He died in AD 675.

Cross the stile and walk ahead down the hill. This lane is sometimes called Nuns Walk, possibly because at some time nuns were living in Bury Bank House on the other side of A51 which you will cross soon.

As you start to go up towards a farm, the wooded hill on your left is Bury Bank. There is an ancient hill fort here, which still has quite impressive ramparts, though they are well covered in bracken. It is strange to think that for a short time this was probably the capital of the ancient kingdom of Mercia. The former name for it was Wulpherecestre – Wulphere's camp. This hill fort was a very significant junction as it was the place where travellers going north either headed north-west for Chester, North Wales and Ireland, or north to Scotland.

As you come towards the farm, keep on the road to the right. The footpath goes over a stile to cross a small field and over another stile to reach the A51.

75

SECTION 3 Stoke to Stafford 23 miles

Take care here as the hedge is close to the road which is often busy. Cross over to the other side and walk down to the Darlaston roundabout where you will cross over the River Trent. Cross carefully over the A34, then turn right and immediately fork left by the George & Dragon which you pass on your right. Walk to the end of the road, turn left and cross over to walk up to a gate where you go through to reach a path up to the canal. Turn right here and walk a mile into Stone which was the original headquarters of the Trent & Mersey Canal. Soon after passing under a railway bridge, the canal bends to the right and you come to Newcastle Road lock with St Dominic's School on the opposite bank. Ahead is a tunnel, where it is easy to imagine a barge horse clopping through, but at this point you leave the canal and turn left along Newcastle Street. If you have time while you are in Stone, you may wish to explore the short attractive stretch of canal here which is not on our route.

Turn left up the next road, Margaret Street, to visit St Dominic's Catholic Church which has a stonework relief depicting the legend of Wulfad and Rufin. If the church is closed you may find one of the sisters at the convent is able to show you round. Phone **01785 812 091** if you wish to check in advance.

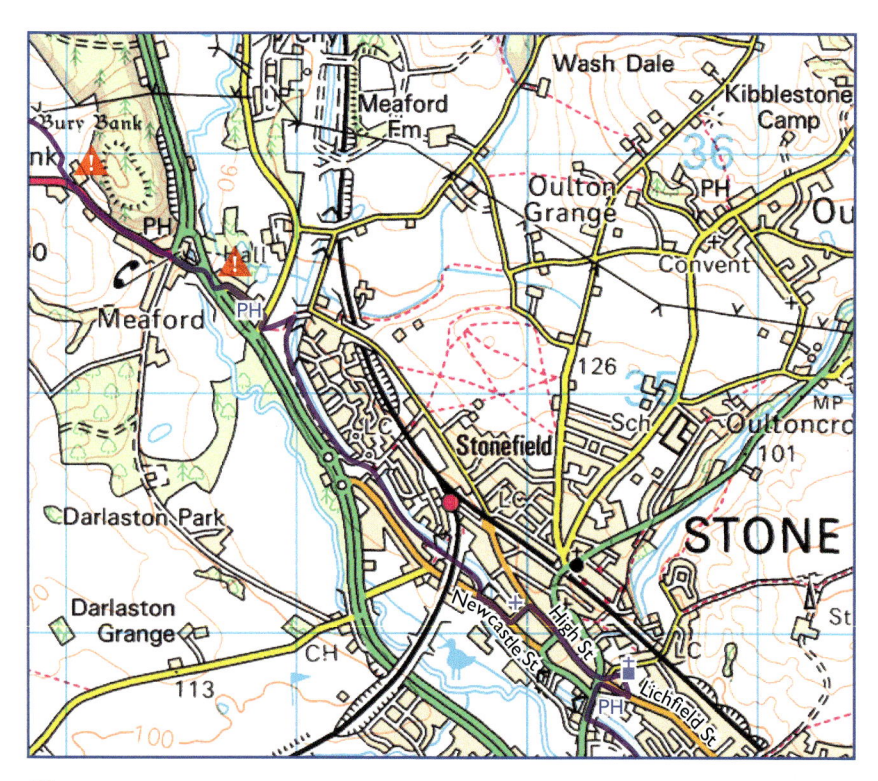

STAGE 10 Tittensor to Stone 4.9 miles

Blessed Dominic Barberi

St Dominic's Roman Catholic Church in Stone is named after the founder of the Dominican order but it also has a strong association with another Dominic who had a most unusual life story. Dominic was an Italian, but he lived and died for England. Born in 1792 in Viterbo in the Papal States, he was the last of eleven children. His father died when he was six and his mother died when he was eleven. In his teens and early twenties he strayed from the faith, but in 1813 he was dramatically converted and at one point as he was praying in a room he heard a voice saying, 'I have chosen you to announce the truths of faith to many nations.' By the following year he gained a strong sense that God was calling him to England. He endeavoured to get to England but all his plans were thwarted. In a letter in 1836, he wrote, 'Is there any hope that I shall cross the sea and convey my body to that island to which 22 years ago I sent my heart?'

At last in 1841 he reached England and in 1842 he entered the Passionist monastery in Aston. Initially he was very unpopular and was called 'The Stuttering Papist' and 'Padre Demenio'. Some people would throw stones at him as he walked between Aston and Stone.

On one occasion he picked up a stone that had been thrown at him, kissed it and put in his pocket. Eventually people changed their views and came to respect him. He was kindly, humorous and children loved him.

He is perhaps best known as the one who received John Henry Newman into the Catholic Church. Newman acknowledged his influence in his conversion. He led many missions and retreats and was also known for his ecumenism, calling other Christians 'brethren'. He died in 1849 of a heart attack while on train near Reading. At his funeral, crowds lined the way from Stone to Aston.

Resuming the walk, at the top of Margaret Street turn right. As you reach Granville Square you will see that some railings at the top of the pedestrianised High Street also depict the legend of Wulfad and Rufin which is the foundational story of Stone. Cross over at the lights into High Street.

SECTION 3 Stoke to Stafford 23 miles

The Legend of Wulfad and Rufin

There are various versions of the legend and the following is a summary of them.

Wulphere, like Penda his father, was a pagan. He wanted to marry Ermenild, a Christian princess from the royal house of Kent, and so to secure his bride he declared himself a Christian. However when he brought Ermenild back to Wulpherecestre (now Bury Bank) he soon reverted to paganism. They had three children: two boys named Wulfad and Rufin and a daughter, Werburgh. The boys were brought up as pagan by their father and Werburgh was raised as a Christian.

As the boys grew up they became very fond of hunting. One day Wulfad was pursuing a white hart. As he was about to shoot, his hand was stayed by a hermit standing by a cave where he was living. The hermit was none other than St Chad. He welcomed Wulfad into his cave and encouraged him to bring his brother Rufin the next day. Wulfad and Rufin secretly visited St Chad many times and in due course were converted to Christianity and baptised.

Meanwhile, King Wulphere had a general called Werebode in his court who desired to marry Werburgh. Wulphere gave his consent, but Werburgh would have none of it as Werebode was a pagan and besides, she was determined to be married to Christ only.

The disgruntled Werebode was seeking revenge for this insult and as he was suspecting the boys, he decided to follow them one day and he spied them in conversation with St Chad. He quickly returned to King Wulphere and reported that the boys had become Christians, adding his own elaboration that they were plotting to overthrow him. Wulphere was so incensed by their betrayal that he ordered the boys to be killed. As they returned to the palace, the boys got wind of their fate and fled, but first Wulfad and then Rufin were slain.

Ermenild and Werburgh took up the bodies of the two boys and as was the custom, they were buried under a pile of stones. This, it is said, is how the township of Stone received its name. Very soon after this, Wulphere was filled with remorse for his dreadful deed and sought and received absolution from St Chad. On this occasion he genuinely renounced his pagan beliefs and became the first Christian King of Mercia. Ermenild and her husband founded a monastery at Stone in honour of their two sons and this became a centre of pilgrimage. Hugh Candidus a monk writing in the 12th century described how a multitude of the infirm and those suffering from diverse weaknesses and of others seeking God ... was accustomed to visit the place and to carry stones thither to the building.

STAGE 10 Tittensor to Stone 4.9 miles

Wulfad and Rufin © David Pott

Walk down the High Street, passing the Crown Hotel on your right. This was once an important staging post for coaches travelling between London and Scotland. You will also pass Cumberland House where the Duke of Cumberland stayed when the Redcoat army were stationed here during the Jacobite Rebellion of 1745.

Cross over at the lights at the bottom of the High Street into Lichfield Street and then first left into Church Street. Turn right up the path to the parish church of St Michael and St Wulfad's.

SECTION 3 Stoke to Stafford 23 miles

Stone Priory and St Michael & St Wulfad's Church

Virtually nothing is known of the original church which existed on this site and was dedicated to St Wulfad. The Augustinian Priory was probably founded in the 1140's by Robert II of Stafford. It covered a wide area between Lichfield Street and the railway line to the north. The priory was originally a daughter house of Kenilworth Priory, but eventually gained independence in 1260. The canons guarded the shrine of St Wulfad which received a steady stream of pilgrims. A license to acquire lands and rent was granted in 1312 "on account of the devotion the king bears to St Wulfad whose body rests in the church of the priory of Stone." In the mid 15th century it was reported that the community was divided by "schisms... insults, hard and unjust words... prolonged malice and wickedness" and subsequent inspections record a turbulent history of the priory until its suppression by Henry VIII in 1537.

The present church was built in 1758 in the early Gothic style in the grounds of the earlier Augustinian Priory The dedication to St Wulfad was restored in 2000. The original box pews are retained. Apart from the east window, the stained glass windows are by Charles Kempe and you can find Wulfad and Rufin on the north aisle. Behind the church there is a classical style mausoleum of Earl Vincent who was Nelson's admiral. There is also a fine 17th century tomb of the Crompton family in the churchyard.

In August 2011, a metal detectorist in Cobham Surrey turned up an object which was identified as a medieval seal matrix from Stone Priory. It depicts the Virgin Mary and the Christ Child and is in remarkably good condition. Money was raised to return it to Stone after about 470 years absence in December 2011 and is now on display in the church. In the ITV documentary, Britain's Secret Treasures, the seal was listed as one out of the 50 most significant objects in the Portable Antiquities scheme to which over 800,000 objects have been submitted.

STAGE 10 Tittensor to Stone 4.9 miles

Seal matrix on right, impression on left © Portable Antiquities Scheme

SECTION 3 Stoke to Stafford 23 miles

Leaving St Michael & St Wulfad's Church, turn left down the path back to Lichfield Street and turn right. Immediately on your right is Priory House. In the basement of the house, which is privately owned, is a vaulted crypt from the Augustinian Priory and in the garden there are a few more ruins. These are the oldest parts of Stone. The practice of carrying stones to Stone was revived here during the inaugural pilgrimage in March 2012. This also takes place in the church. It may be possible to see the crypt by arrangement with the owner, Timothy Gillow, by phoning him on 01785 818 688 or e-mail thegillows@yahoo.co.uk

Cross over Lichfield Street and go ahead towards the lights, passing shops on your left. Turn left into Earl St Vincent Square, so named after Stone's famous son Admiral John Jervis, a colleague of Lord Nelson who became Earl St Vincent after defeating the Spanish off Cape St Vincent in 1797. Cross Abbey Street, passing the Swan Inn on your left. You soon reach the canal again and resume the journey south on the towpath on the western bank. After walking a little over a mile you pass under the A51 and shortly after you come to Aston Bridge where you turn off to the right (east). Cross the River Trent. After 100 yards turn left into the churchyard of St Saviour's church. When you leave the church you will see a driveway ahead of you leading past a chapel to Aston Hall. Take the tarmaced way immediately to the left of the drive. Keep the wall on your right. It leads round to a pleasant stretch skirting round Aston Hall. This path turns right and left into Aston Lane.

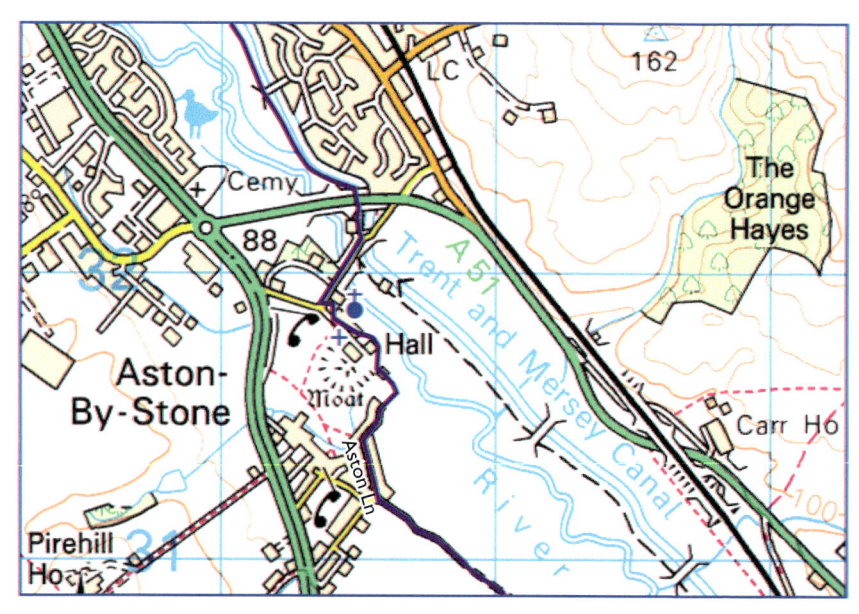

STAGE 11 Stone to Sandon 4.9 miles

Aston Hall

Aston Hall has had a close association with Roman Catholicism for over a thousand years. It belonged to the Fitzpaynes, the Stanleys (Earls of Derby) and at the time of the Reformation, the Heveninghams. They managed to retain a priest who was usually a Jesuit. A saying has been handed down: There shall always be a priest at Aston, as long as the wind blows and water flows, and night follows day.

Aston Hall is now a home for retired priests. It was here in 1839 that the bones of St Chad were found in a box under the altar of the chapel. These relics had been kept secretly since the Reformation and for a while had been with the Fitzherbert family in nearby Swynnerton Hall where the key to the box was found with an explanatory label. The bones were taken to the new cathedral in Birmingham and are housed there in a specially built chapel.

Apart from Blessed Dominic Barberi mentioned on page 73, another former resident of Aston Hall was St Charles of Mount Argon (1821–1893). He was born in Belgium and became a

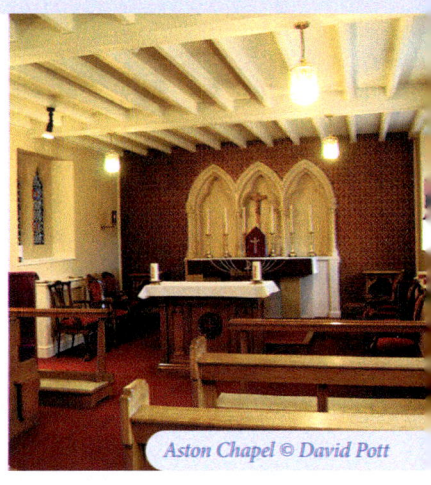

Aston Chapel © David Pott

Passionist Priest in 1850. He left for England in 1850 and was at Aston from 1852 to 1854. It was in Stone that he first was drawn to the poverty-stricken Irish and in 1857 he went to the Monastery of Mount Argon in Dublin where he gained a great reputation as a healer. He was canonised by Pope Benedict XVI in 2007.

To see if it is possible to visit this very beautiful chapel, please ring **Deacon Trevor** beforehand on **01785 812001** or email him on **deacontrevor@hotmail.co.uk**.

At the bottom of Aston Lane where the road turns right continue straight on down the track. This soon leads out to two large fields which you are to cross over. Carry on over a stile into a nature reserve, with a lake to your left. Cross a bridge over the River Trent and another bridge over the canal and you will arrive in Burston.

SECTION 3 Stoke to Stafford 23 miles

Burston Pond © David Pott

Burston is a delightful village with an attractive row of cottages beside a millpond.

St Rufin's Church at the end of the row of cottages is a very unassuming building which blends inconspicuously into the scene. It was built in 1859 and replaced an older chapel. It is often open, but if not, the key should be available at cottage no 9. The first chapel was most probably close to the canal and it seems that the last stones were probably cleared and used in the construction of the canal in the 1770s.

After passing the pond on your left and a small car par park on your right, take the turning on your right down a lane which will soon return you to the next bridge over the canal. Before you continue your southward journey on the canal towpath

Ancient Chapel Stone © David Pott

take a look back at the field on the eastern side of the canal where a clump of trees hides a well, which is known as St Rufin's or St Chad's Well. Hereabouts also was the original chapel, no doubt often visited by pilgrims in the Middle Ages.

STAGE 11 Stone to Sandon 4.9 miles

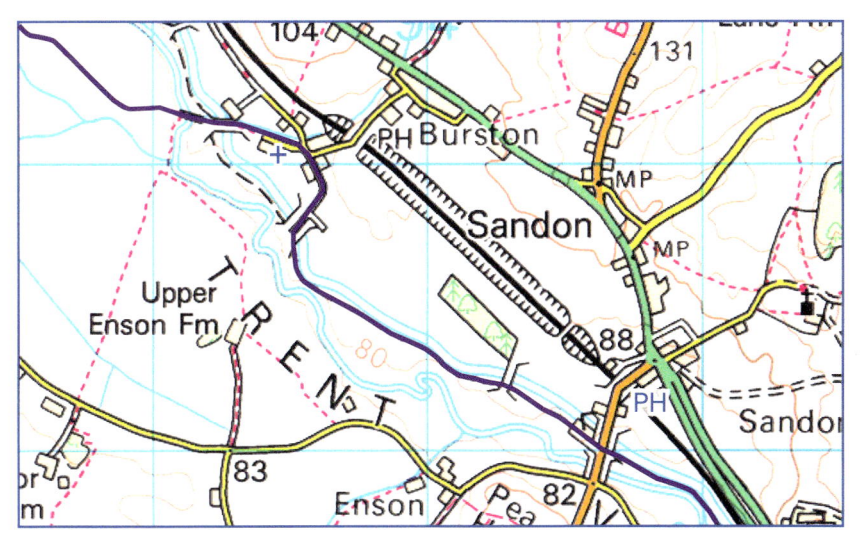

Swans & Cattle © Candice Smith

Continue under bridge no. 84. When you reach the next bridge (no. 83) the canal goes under the B5066. The Dog & Doublet pub at Sandon is 200 metres to the left.

85

SECTION 3 Stoke to Stafford 23 miles

Continue along the canal and at the next ornate bridge (no. 82), built in the 18th century, turn right up to the road and left towards the village of Salt soon passing Casey Cottage and two seats on the left hand side giving you a choice of views either east or west. To the east is an urn-topped column commemorating William Pitt in Sandon Park erected in 1806.

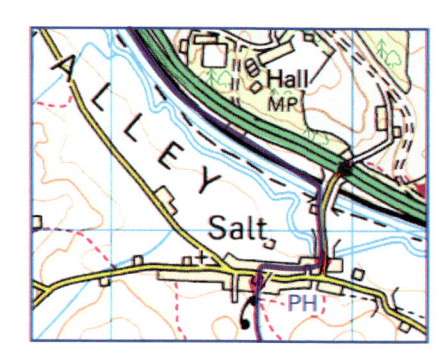

Salt

The village of Salt is listed in the Doomsday Book (1087) as 'Selte', which implies the existence of a salt pit or salt works which may have existed as long ago as Roman times.

The Hollybush Inn is thought to be the second licensed pub in England. Licensing began in the reign of Charles II (1660–1685).

The present building dates from the 17th century, but a public house is believed to have existed here since 1190.

Beside the Hollybush is a private residence which was formerly Salt Railway Station on the Stafford Uttoxeter line which was closed in 1951.

At the T-junction in Salt turn right, passing the attractive thatched Hollybush Inn. Proceed 250 yards and turn left into Brooke Lane opposite a telephone kiosk. Straight ahead is a gate with a metal kissing gate. After about 150 yards, look out for the path going diagonally right through a crop field. Pass through another kissing gate which may mention that there is a bull in the field. If he is there, he will be more interested in his harem than you. Proceed up the hill and before going through the next kissing gate, take a look back at the view of Salt with Sandon Hall behind. Go a few yards through some woodland and another kissing gate into a large field, sometimes slightly boggy after heavy rain. Walk on, heading slightly right and through a kissing gate into the wood. The path soon meets a wider woodland track where you turn left and soon reach crosspaths. Carry straight on following the field boundary with the hedge on your right. The footpath will lead you to the right of the MOD property ahead. Incongruously placed behind the chain link fencing, but well worth pausing

STAGE 12 Sandon to Stafford 6.3 miles

to read, you will find a memorial stone and an excellent interpretation panel about the Civil War Battle of Hopton Heath, fought here on 19th March 1643. It was erected on 19th March 2010 by the Military Historical Society. Carry straight on into next field to meet a road where you turn right and after 150 yards turn left into Hopton. It has won a number of best kept village awards. There is an attractive descent through sandstone banks and a little green with a bench. Turn left into King's Drive which soon turns left. At the end of the road you will find the footpath on the right. Cross the stile and you will see your next destination, the wooded top of Beacon Hill straight ahead of you.

Continue straight downhill, crossing a small stream and over a stile onto a wide farm track. Where the main track turns left, keep straight ahead up to the wood on a greener track, keeping the hedge on the left. When you reach the wood, turn right. There are fine views with the Wrekin 25 miles away to the west and Stafford with Cannock Chase behind it as you circle round. As you walk down and pass the end of the wood and a stile on your left, look for a path veering off right towards Beacon Farm. Go though a kissing gate (this field boundary may not be marked if you have an Explorer map) and cross the next field. Cross over the farm track and go through the kissing gate. Cross the field, bearing right towards the farm and through

Canal bridge Salt © David Pott

the next kissing gate. Carry on down the track with a house on your left and barn conversions on your right. The track becomes a tarmac road with cattle grids and kissing gates which eventually meets the busy A513. Cross with care.

Turn right along the cycle path and footway and after crossing a stream, take the next path turning into a housing estate. Turn right here through the trees and keep on along Portal Road for 300 yards until you see Trenchard Avenue on your left. Walk along the footway on the left hand side until you come to a recreation ground on your right which you cross diagonally to Cambridge Street.

SECTION 3 Stoke to Stafford 23 miles

Turn left here and you will soon find allotments on your right. Take the footpath through the middle of the allotments to the far end and then turn left towards the traffic lights. At the lights, cross over Corporation Street into Crooked Bridge Road. At the end of that road turn left into Goal Road with Stafford Prison on your left. When you arrive at the A34 (Queensway), cross at the lights over to the pedestrianised Gaolgate Street.

As you walk down Gaolgate Street, you will soon reach the Market Square with the Shire Hall Gallery to your left. Take St Mary's Passage after Boots on your right to visit the Collegiate Church of St Mary. As you walk round on the western side, you will see the outline of St Bertelin's Chapel. The entrance is on the southern side of the church.

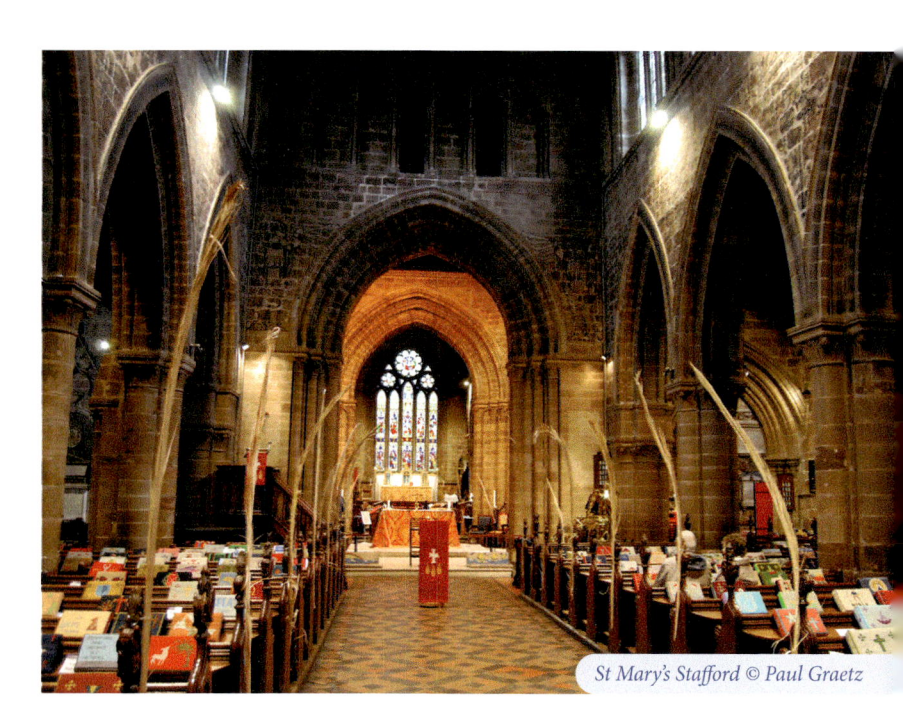

St Mary's Stafford © Paul Graetz

STAGE 12 Sandon to Stafford 6.3 miles

St Mary's Collegiate Church

The earliest references to a church in Stafford are from the 10th century and mention a wooden building on the site of St Bertelin's Chapel. The foundations can be seen at the west end of St Mary's today. This was replaced with a stone structure c. AD 1000. This building appears to have been largely rebuilt in the 13th and 14th centuries with the addition of a clerestory and south aisle. Some stonework in the nave of St Mary's is said to be Norman in origin but the building as it stands today appears to be the result of a total rebuild in the early 13th century.

The oldest object in the church is a font dated from Norman times but which has unusual Byzantine features. Until 1593 the octagonal tower was topped by a spire said to be one of the highest in England. A ferocious storm that year blew it down, causing major damage to the south transept and the spire was never rebuilt.

St Mary's has had a colourful history. A pitched battle was fought within the church in 1258 when the Bishop of Lichfield – Roger de Meuland – entered it by force of arms, breaking open the doors at the head of an armed troop to exert his authority over the Royal Peculiar. Sadly, blood was shed and some canons were wounded. During the Civil War it is said that Prince Rupert, who was residing briefly at the Ancient High House in 1642, took pot shots at the weathervane on St Mary's tower, apparently hitting the tail of the cockerel twice. When Stafford fell to the Parliamentary forces eight months later, the church became a barracks and stables.

By 1777 St Mary's was in such poor state of repair that it had to be closed. Some works were carried out but by 1837 the church was once more in a dilapidated condition. A complete restoration commenced in 1842 and was completed in 1844. A. W. N. Pugin pronounced the project to be 'the best restoration … in modern times'.

The church is open from 10am to 3pm between April and September and from 11am to 2pm from October to March. If you wish to find out if it is possible to visit outside these times, please telephone the parish office on **01785 258 511**.

SECTION 3 Stoke to Stafford 23 miles

Ancient High House © Stafford Borough Council

When you have completed your visit, turn left and walk through the alley ahead to return to the pedestrianised street now called Greengate Street. On the corner is the Ancient High House, England's largest timber-framed town house. Turn right and immediately on your left you reach St Chad's Church.

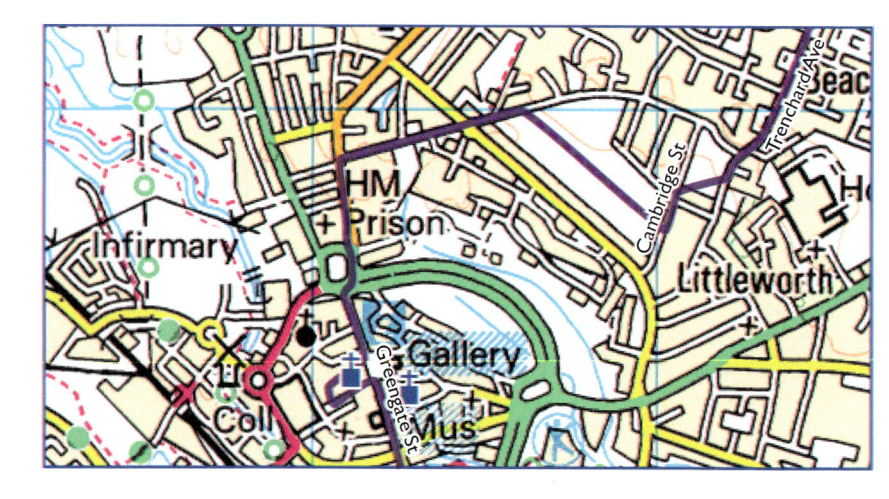

STAGE 12 Sandon to Stafford 6.3 miles

St Chad's Church

Dating from about 1150, this church is the oldest building in Stafford and contains some of the finest Norman stone carvings in the Midlands. The church was sadly neglected in the 17th and 18th centuries but was restored in the 18th century principally by George Gilbert Scott who donated the statue of St Chad's in the central niche of the west front. Outside, beside the modern war memorial cross, is the base of a medieval churchyard cross known as St Chad's Cross with the inscription in Latin which means 'what the forbidden fruit fatal did for man, that blood undid which from Christ's body ran.' Within the church, the nave arcades feature massive round pillars and the tower arch has carvings that show an eastern influence. In the chancel there is a carving of a 'Green Man' and there is an inscription to Orm, the founder of the church.

St Chad's Stafford © Andrew Baker

STAGE 13 Stafford to Milford 4.6 miles

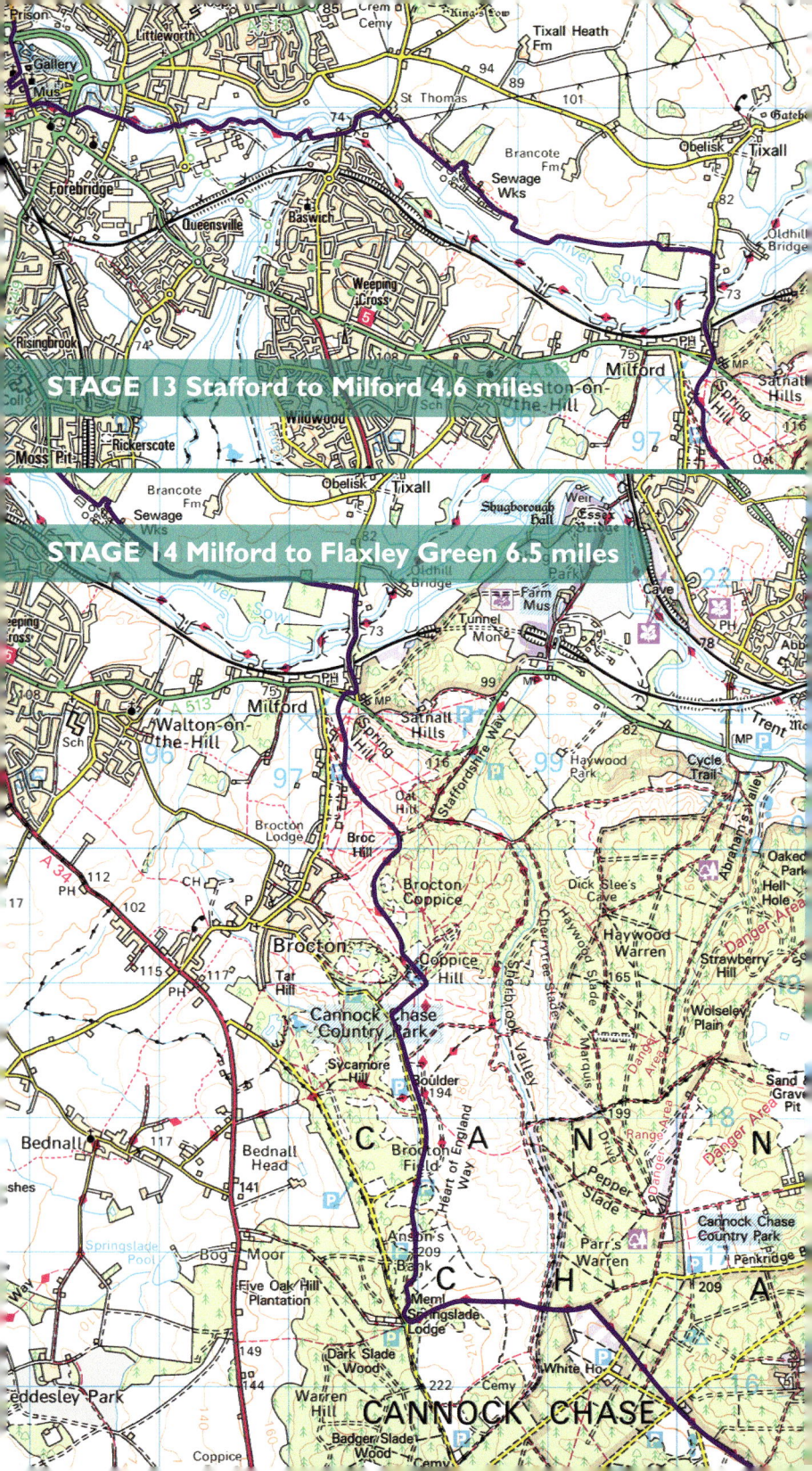

STAGE 14 Milford to Flaxley Green 6.5 miles

STAGE 15 Flaxley Green to Cannock Wood 3.2 miles

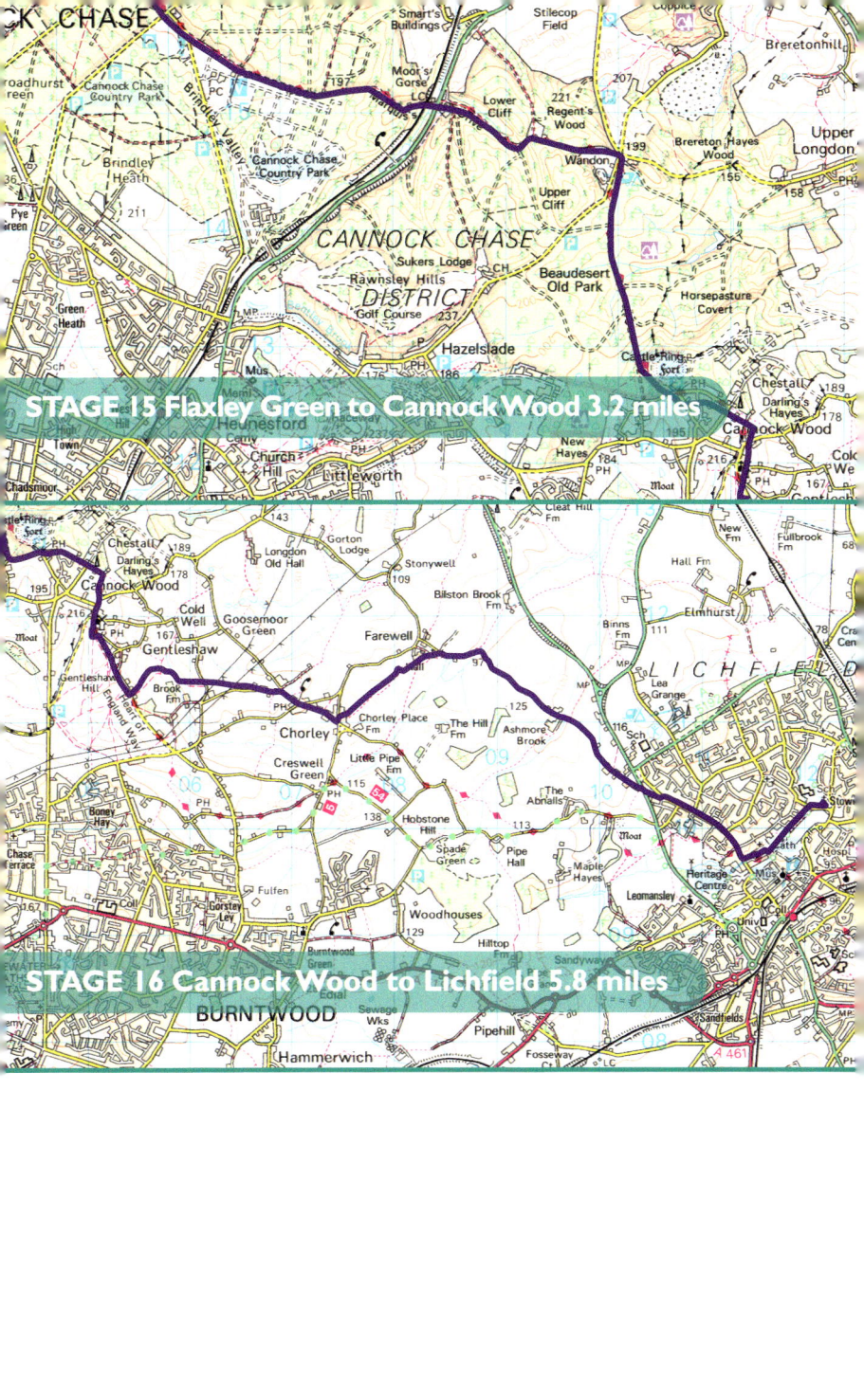

STAGE 16 Cannock Wood to Lichfield 5.8 miles

SECTION 4 Stafford to Lichfield 20 miles

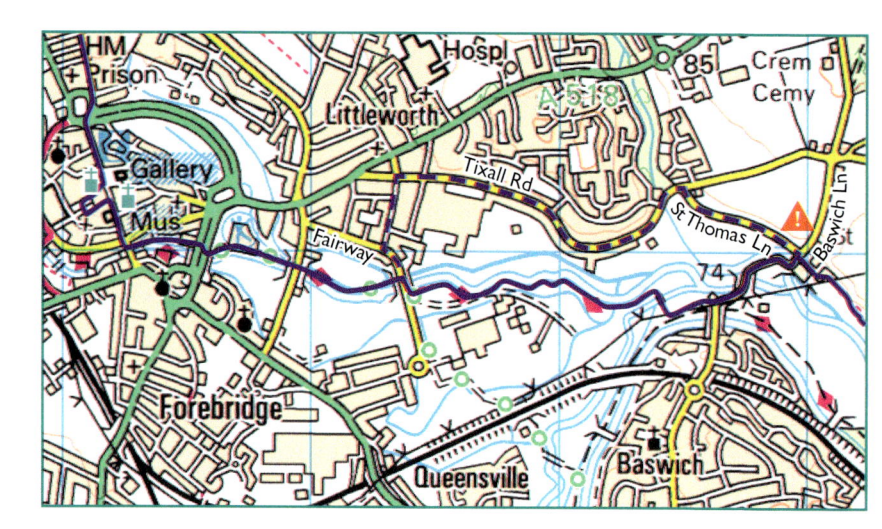

After leaving St Chad's Church, turn left and continue down Greengate Street, then cross over by Nationwide Building Society into Bridge Street. When you reach the bridge, turn left onto the path and proceed on the northern side of the River Sow heading east. You will pass the council offices and an Asda supermarket. This is the last shop that is directly on the route until you reach Lichfield.

When you reach the second bridge at Fairway, cross the river to the south side. There now follows a pleasant stretch following the meanders of the River Sow, gradually leaving the sounds of Stafford behind.
Eventually the path leaves the river as it bends to the left, to go over a bridge crossing a marshy patch and soon over a second bridge crossing the River Penk. Cross the field and go over the stile into Baswich Lane where you turn left. Baswich Lane can be very busy and if you would like to avoid this you can use the new Two Waters Way and St Thomas Lane to the north as a longer but safer alternative.

Alternative route

The section between Fairway and Baswich Lane can be subject to flooding, so if that is the case turn left at Fairway. After passing the Kingston Centre on your right, turn right into Dartmouth Street and after 200 yards turn right into Tixall Road and follow it for two thirds of a mile then turn right into St Thomas Lane. Cross over Baswich Lane to resume the Two Saints Way. .

STAGE 13 Stafford to Milford 4.6 miles

Bridge near Baswich Lane © Candice Smith

St Thomas Priory

In 1170 Thomas à Becket was assassinated at Canterbury Cathedral. Three years later he was canonised and it is a mark of his popularity that only one year later in 1174, a priory was established here and dedicated to him. In 1182, Richard Peche, who had been a friend of Thomas, resigned as Bishop of Coventry and Lichfield and became an Augustinian canon here shortly before his death. The priory was a small one, but was also very wealthy, which was unusual for a religious house in Staffordshire. Henry IV stayed at the priory in 1403. It is likely that pilgrims destined for St Thomas' shrine at Canterbury would have lodged here.

Priories were subject to inspection and one taken in 1518 recorded that prior's servants did not show proper respect to the ordinary canons and that there were too many hunting dogs! The priory was dissolved in 1538.

Mill pond St Thomas Priory © Candice Smith

SECTION 4 Stafford to Lichfield 20 miles

Cross over the River Sow again and turn right when you reach St Thomas Priory Farm where some of the stones from the former priory have been used for modern houses. After passing those, turn right on a track which passes the 17th-century farmhouse. The garden includes a stretch of priory wall and beyond is the Mill Pond. The owner Mr John Martin may be able to show you this site. Please contact him by emailing dfoss@metronet.co.uk or telephoning 01785 223 748.

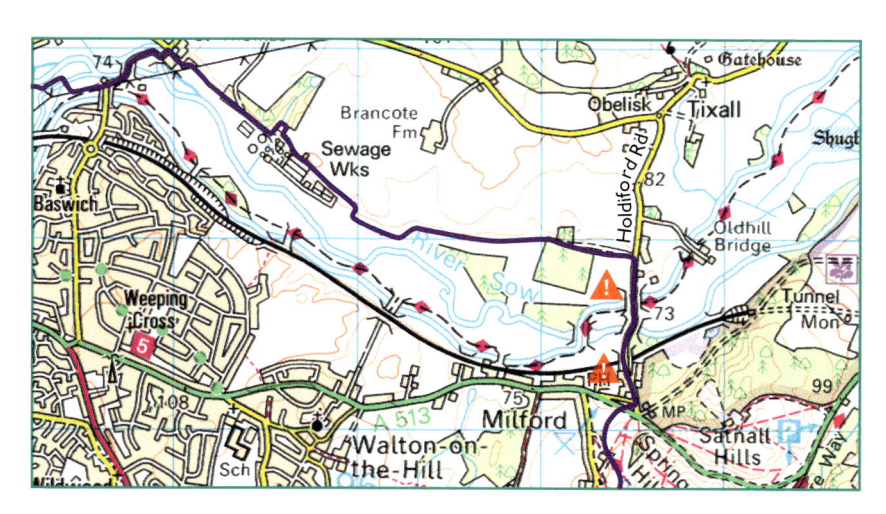

Alternative route

Two miles beyond this point, there is a stretch of road with three bridges which requires special care. You can avoid the first of the bridges by taking the Staffordshire and Worcestershire Canal. If you prefer to take this alternative, return along the way you have just come until you reach the canal where you turn left. After 2.5 miles you will reach Holdiford Road where you turn right to rejoin the route.

The track leads along a pleasant green lane, which soon goes right towards the river, but you go ahead over a stile and you will join a road towards the sewage works. The nature of your experience here may be determined by the wind direction!

STAGE 13 Stafford to Milford 4.6 miles

View towards Cannock Chase © Peter Graysmith

Just before the main entrance, turn left where you are corralled around the northern side of the works before crossing a stile into a field with the sewage works still on your right. After you leave the sewage works cross a stile into a field. Go down here, keeping below the hill with a few pine trees on your left then cross the field to the stile. Continue across the next field and through a gate with woodland on your right. Cross the next field into a short stretch of woodland. Twenty yards before a gate, look for a path on the right that runs parallel to the main track through the wood (This path you are supposed to use to the south of the main track is often overgrown - you may find you have to stick to the main track through two gates here). This soon exits over a stile into a field. Keep by the hedge and rejoin the track across the field to the stile onto Holdiford Road where you turn right. Take special care on this stretch which crosses three bridges over the canal, the River Sow and the railway to reach Milford. It can be very busy at times and where there is no grass verge before the canal bridge. This bridge is narrow and humpbacked so it is advisable to approach with care and only cross when you can see and hear no traffic.

After you cross the river, take the pavement and you soon reach Milford. The entrance to Shugborough Hall is close by on the western side of Holdiford Road and you may well want to walk the mile or so to visit it.

SECTION 4 Stafford to Lichfield 20 miles

Cross over the A513 and the green to the car park on the other side. On the left hand side of the car park is the footpath you take up onto Cannock Chase where the Two Saints Way joins the Heart of England Way.

Cannock Chase

Cannock Chase is the remnant of what was a huge forest – Cannock Forest – in which Henry II hunted. It stretched from Wolverhampton to Tamworth and from Walsall to the Trent. In 1290 the hunting rights passed on to the Bishops of Lichfield and it was then called the Bishop's Chase, chase being the medieval name for a hunting area. They hunted fallow and red deer which are still found here.

Cannock Chase, at 26 square miles, is England's smallest Area of Outstanding Natural Beauty (AONB).

Cannock Chase © Teeranlall Ramgopal

When you come to a small pond, keep it to your left and immediately after branch off left up onto a narrower path. You will soon find you are going up a cutting. This section follows the course of the Tackeroo Railway which was built in 1915 to serve the training camps on the Chase during World War 1. Continue onwards, passing Mere Pits on your right. Keep on the embankment circling round right and then left to parallel another path in the valley on your right till the paths join shortly before you reach Freda's Grave car park at Coppice Hill. Continue straight over at the car park. As you come to a more open stretch of the Chase where the trees thin out, fork right. Before long you share the route for a few yards with the Staffordshire Way, until the point where a trig point is

STAGE 14 Milford to Flaxley Green 6.5 miles

Tackeroo © David Pott

seen on your right. Our route continues ahead, but you may like to see a glacial boulder which stands on a plinth behind the trig point. This 'erratic' was carried here during the Ice Ages all the way from southwest Scotland.

As you continue, you will now see an upland marsh pool called Womere on your right – there are very few of these in the Midlands. Local legend has it that it is bottomless, but in fact it is a shallow pond. When you come to the next path junction at a clump of birch trees, fork right to arrive at another car park. Walk towards the tarmac road, but take the path to the left before you reach it. This part of the Chase is called Anson's Bank after the Anson family of Shugborough Hall. The most famous member of the family was Admiral George Anson who sailed round the world in 1740. His brother Thomas planted pine trees in prominent spots between here and Millford to commemorate his feat. A few yards off to your right you should find a toposcope which indicates highlights of the view which could at one time be appreciated from here, but now trees have obscured it.

Womere © Graham Walker

99

SECTION 4 Stafford to Lichfield 20 miles

The path comes out to a tarmac road (Camp Road) and to Springslade Lodge tearoom, a good place to pause for refreshment. Turn left here and you will come to the Katyn Memorial.

The Katyn Memorial

This memorial was built in 1979 by the Anglo-Polish Society to commemorate the murder of 14,000 Polish army officers and intellectuals in the Katyn Forest in 1940. Many Poles came here again for the 60th anniversary following the tragic death of President Lech Kaczynski and 95 other Poles in an air crash as they were about to attend commemorations at Katyn. Half a mile to the south of here is the German War Memorial to all the Germans who died in Britain in both world wars.

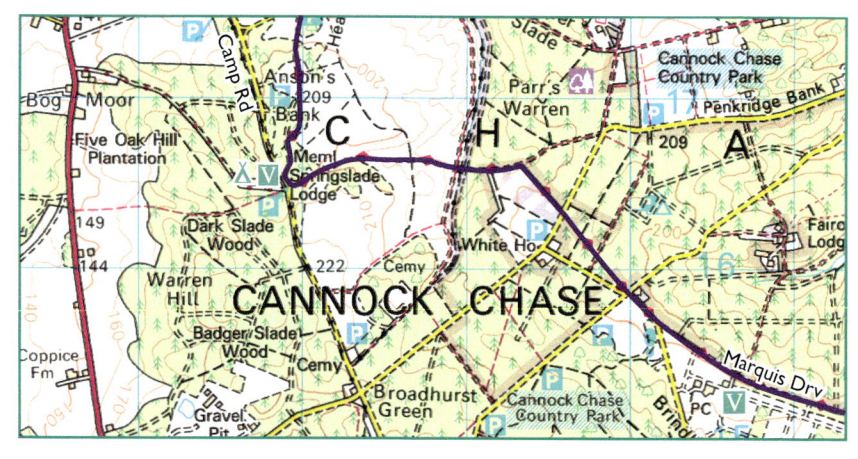

Memorial © Candice Smith

STAGE 14 Milford to Flaxley Green 6.5 miles

Continue on eastwards soon coming to another open stretch of heath before crossing the Sherbrook Valley with more pine woodland on the left. After walking about 400 yards uphill fork right with a younger plantation now on your left. A further 400 yards brings you to another road which you cross straight over. In the next section you continue straight on with two right and left dog legs as you cross other paths through the wood. You now arrive at a cottage called Flints Corner. Keep it on your left as you continue ahead and fork left. You are now on Marquis Drive which you will be following for nearly three miles. It is named after the Marquis of Anglesey.

Sherbrook Valley © Graham Walker

Marquis of Anglesey

William Henry Paget, Marquis of Anglesey and also Earl of Uxbridge and Beaudesert, was an interesting character. He was second-in-command to the Duke of Wellington at the Battle of Waterloo (1815) and in a famous exchange after a cannonball had blown the Marquis' leg off, he said to Wellington, 'By God sir, I've lost my leg!' to which he replied, 'By God sir, so you have!' Later as the remains of his leg were being amputated he was extraordinarily calm and commented dryly, 'The knives appear somewhat blunt.' Later he said, 'Who would not lose a leg for such a victory!' When he returned home, 10,000 tenants are said to have welcomed the hero home and hauled his carriage by hand from Lichfield to Beaudesert. He had eight children by his first wife, Lady Caroline Villiers and when she died (exhausted?) ten more by his second wife Lady Charlotte Wellesley.

On your right, after passing an open green and the Burma Star Memorial Copse, you may wish to visit the Cannock Chase Visitor Centre. The route continues straight on down the drive, passing a barrier. Just before tarmac gives way to gravel there is an interpretation panel about RAF Hednesford which occupied a large amount of land here in the Second World War. The hill ahead of you is called Kit Bag Hill and it was considered a rough deal if your quarters were up there! The camp stretched from the visitor centre to the top of Kitbag Hill.

The path now descends to cross a railway and the A460 near Flaxley Green.

SECTION 4 Stafford to Lichfield 20 miles

Continue straight over, then up the hill passing Moors Goose Pumping Station on your right and with a stream on your left. When you come to a fork, turn left, crossing the stream and with a pond on your right. A path comes in from Miflins Valley on your left before you pass a house also on your left. Continue uphill till you reach a road junction and the end of Marquis Drive.

Turn right here and after a few yards turn left up a forest track, then right to parallel the road. When the path once again comes close to the road, swing left heading down into a valley with the view ahead of the steepest climb on the route. This area of the Chase is called Beaudesert and in medieval times, when the Chase was called the Bishop's Chase, it was at the heart of the forest.

Cross over two fords with a pond to the right of the first one, then keep straight ahead on a narrower path to join a wider one heading straight uphill. At the next junction where the main path bears right, keep straight on uphill. Just before you reach the top of the hill a marker indicates the fork left along a narrower track to Castle Ring Fort. The route skirts the western edge of the fort but you will probably want to go to the top to enjoy the view particularly to the east with Rugeley Power Station prominent. Follow the rampart round to the south-western corner and the car park there.

Castle Ring Hill Fort

Castle Ring is at 801 Feet (244 metres) the highest point on Cannock Chase. This hillfort probably dates from around 150 BC and it was probably occupied until AD 500. It would have been used by the first Iron Age farming communities as a place to flee to from the attacks of other tribes or pirates and to store grain. It would have had a prominent wooden stockade on the inner rampart and a well-fortified gate to protect the entrance.

Opposite the car park is the Park Gate Inn. Leave the car park and turn left immediately to walk down Holly Hill Road. (The first track on your left leads into the Beaudesert Park Scout Camp, but you may only enter if you have received prior permission.)

STAGE 15 Flaxley Green to Cannock Wood 3.2 miles

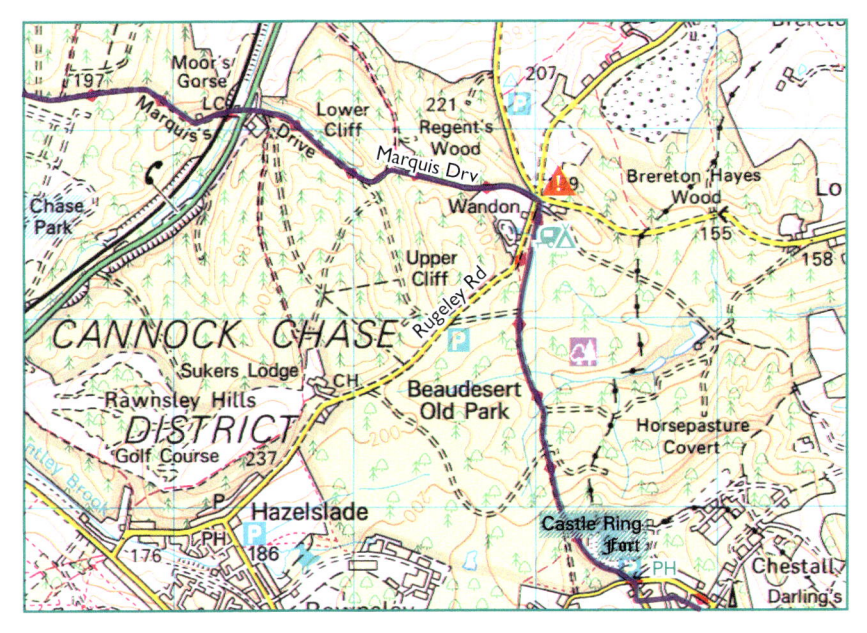

View from Castle Ring © Tim Saxton

103

SECTION 4 Stafford to Lichfield 20 miles

Beaudesert Scout Camp and Hall

General access to Beaudesert is not permitted due to the constraints imposed by the protection measures for children and young people and there are no rights of way within the site. However access for pilgrims may be possible in accordance with the Trust's managed access policy by contacting the estate manager of the Beaudesert Trust beforehand.
Email **info@beaudesert.org** or telephone **01543 682 278**.

Beaudesert and the Paget family have important links with Lichfield Cathedral and Burton Abbey. Beaudesert Hall, the former medieval house of the Bishops of Coventry and Lichfield, dates from 1190 and incorporated an episcopal chapel. After the Dissolution of the Monasteries in 1536, Henry VIII confiscated the Bishop's lands and gave them to Sir William Paget who became the 1st Baron of Beaudesert. Later it was constructed as an Elizabethan mansion by the 3rd Baron of Beaudesert.

After entering into the scout camp go straight ahead, passing a walled garden on your right and keep on till you arrive at some low buildings on your right. Report to reception where you will be asked to sign in. You may receive a map. An audio trail which tells you about the history of the site is also available. Walk to the central avenue and head downhill passing two gateways. On your left is a stream and you will be able to make out the remains of old water features there. You will then arrive at the ruins of Beaudesert Hall.

Ruins of Beaudesert Hall © Candice Smith

Go up the last flight of steps near the east end of the hall and pass some old sweet chestnut trees before reaching a fine toposcope installed in 2011 to indicate the extent and position of the lands taken from the church and given to William Paget. If you do visit Beaudesert, this will be the first place that you see Lichfield Cathedral. In the traditions of pilgrimage, this would be the natural place to pause and rejoice at the sight of the destination and to give thanks for a safe journey.

Take the higher path at the upper rim of the valley as you make your way back to the reception. After reporting back there, leave by the way you came in.

STAGE 15 Flaxley Green to Cannock Wood 3.2 miles

At the end of Holly Hill Road you will see the main entrance to Beaudesert Park on your left. Reflections Gardens, which will be of interest to pilgrims, is down this road, but the route itself continues on the path ahead between the railings with a reservoir on the right and woodland on the left.

Reflections Gardens

*Walking in the Reflections Gardens at Little Hayes, the home of Revd Christine and John Polhill, is an appropriate pilgrimage experience. It can be found on the left-hand side after a ten-minute walk from the entrance. There are five small gardens which link environmental themes with spiritual themes based on Ignatian exercises. The gardens are unconventional and call forth a response. There is also a free standing unit called the Hermitage which provides accommodation for an individual or couple. There is no charge but visitors are invited to make a donation to the Rivendell Trust, a charity that funds the work. If you wish to make a visit or arrange to stay overnight ring **01543 674 474** or email **polhill@reflectiongardens.org.uk**. Further information can be found at **www.reflectiongardens.org.uk**.*

The path past the reservoir comes out onto a tarmac lane where you turn right, keeping the railings of the reservoir on your right. As you walk along this lane, look left for views of the famous three spires of Lichfield Cathedral – the Ladies of the Vale.

When the lane bends to the left, continue straight on along the short path through the trees to the road. The centre of Cannock Wood, where there is a bus service, is to your right along Buds Road, but the route continues straight ahead, passing Gentleshaw Primary school and the church on your left.

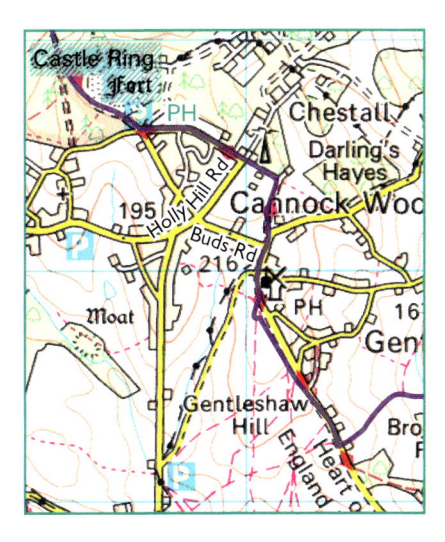

SECTION 4 Stafford to Lichfield 20 miles

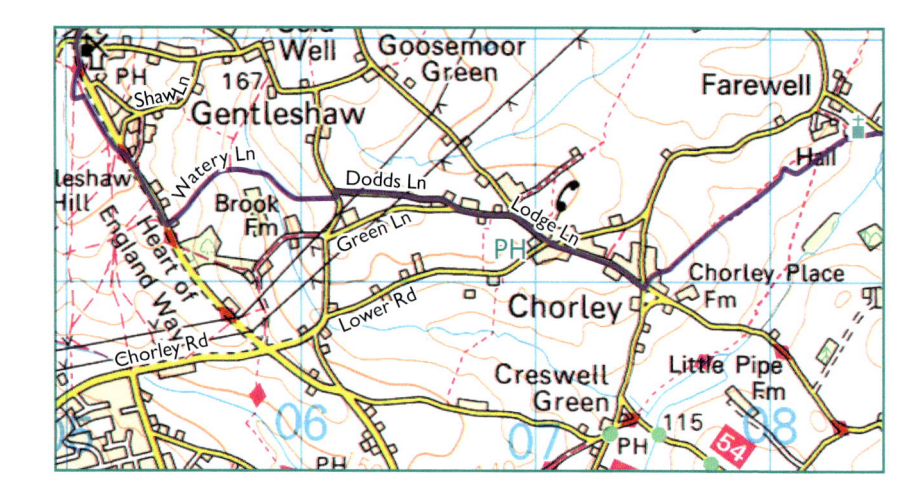

You now reach Gentleshaw Common on your right. There are several paths at this point, but take the middle one for 150 yards until you come out of the woods to enjoy a good view to the south-west across Burntwood. Turn left here, crossing a cross paths before turning right on the path parallel with the road. Keep on the path, passing Shaw Lane and Greenhills Nurseries on your left and then take the next path on your left to Windy Ridge Nurseries. At this point you leave the Heart of England Way.

Cross over to the path with Windy Ridge Nursery on your right and go down into a wooded area which broadens then narrows again near the bottom. Turn right along the path here which is called Watery Lane. You will soon cross a culverted stream where it can be rather muddy. Continue uphill, enjoying the pleasant view to your right of Brook Farm and a statue of a deer near a duck pond. At the top of the lane cross over a road into the narrow Dodds Lane between holly hedgerows.

Alternative route

After very heavy rain Watery Lane may be difficult, so if this is the case, continue south from Windy Ridge Nursery along the eastern edge of Gentleshaw Common until you come to crossroads where you turn left into Chorley Road. Pass roads on your right and left and continue into Lower Road which leads to Chorley where you resume the Two Saints Way at the Malt and Shovel pub and turn right.

STAGE 16 Cannock Wood to Lichfield 5.8 miles

View from Watery Lane © David Pott

Dodd's Lane joins Green Lane where you continue ahead. After 200 yards you come to a T-junction where you turn right into Lodge Lane. You soon reach the flat x-shaped crossroads in Chorley with the Malt Shovel on your right. Cross straight over and after about 300 yards as the road descends, you come to another crossroads where you turn left. Take the footpath on your right to the left of the village hall. Go through a gate and turn right behind the hall to cross over the stile and turn left. *(NB It is curious that this is the correct right of way and if the community hall gate is locked, as it sometimes is, you will have to go on the more obvious path to the right of the hall!)* Cross over the next stile by a gate and you will be able to see your next destination of Farewell straight ahead of you. Follow the signs through the fields, passing a pond with an island on your right. Pass close by the hall on your left to a gateway and straight on to St Bartholomew's Church. Take the footpath to the right of the church. It passes diagonally towards the bottom right-hand corner of the field. Forty yards before reaching the corner, turn left at an electricity pole to reveal a kissing gate in the thick holly hedge. Go over the stile and turn right into Cross in Hand Lane.

SECTION 4 Stafford to Lichfield 20 miles

Farewell and Cross in Hand Lane

Some say that the name Farewell derives from pilgrims parting company after visiting Lichfield at this point, but the more likely origin is the more obvious one of 'clear spring'.

A religious house was founded here by Roger de Clinton, Bishop of Lichfield in the 12th century as a place for hermits and monks, but it soon became a nunnery. It was later to become a Benedictine priory. It was dissolved in 1527 when the prioress and four remaining nuns were transferred to other nunneries.

The parish church of St Bartholomew is thought to be built on the site of the priory chapel. Apart from the stone chancel, it was completely rebuilt in 1740, but altar rails, the glass in the east window and the miserere stalls are from the 13th century. Another restoration of the building took place in 1848.

Cross in Hand Lane is so called because pilgrims who had sought hospitality here would carry a small cross in the hand with them to meditate on as they approached the shrine of St Chad. Farewell Hall nearby was built in the 17th century.

St Bartholomew Farewell © Candice Smith

STAGE 16 Cannock Wood to Lichfield 5.8 miles

Cross in Hand Lane is a quintessential English lane passing through pleasant farmland. This lane of almost two miles is generally quiet except during the rush hour. Mill Farm with its small lake on the right is on the site of the mill that existed in the time of the priory. There are a number of listed buildings along the way and in places the lane is carved out between Keuper sandstone banks.

As you come to the bottom of the last hill before Lichfield look out for a small cave on your left opposite a house. Local lore has it that it was used by candle sellers in the days of medieval pilgrimage.

Just before the lane reaches the A51 it turns left. Ignore the turn and continue in the same direction over the triangle of grass to reach the main road. Cross the busy road with care to the verge on the opposite side. Cross over the verge to re-enter Cross in Hand Lane which continues for another 150 yards on the other side of the A51. At the end turn left and right into Beacon Street, but before you do so, notice the Pinfold on your left. This was a place where stray cattle were rounded up and kept by the 'pinner' before the enclosures. The city council still appoints two pinners and a pinlock keeper every year!

As you walk down Beacon Street you can perhaps imagine yourself joining in spirit with the many other pilgrims who would have trod this way towards the cathedral. There are a number of interesting buildings on Beacon Street, including a house which was originally built in 1504 as a hospitality house for women. After passing Erasmus Darwin House, turn left to go to the cathedral.

After you have visited the cathedral, turn left and go round the south side and then turn right down Dam Street and immediately left along Reeve Lane. Immediately beyond a cross-path, the lane splits into two parallel lanes. Take the right-hand lane leading to Stowe Pool.

Lichfield Cathedral from Stowe Pool © David Pott

SECTION 4 Stafford to Lichfield 20 miles

Pilgrims in Lichfield © Candice Smith

You will see St Chad's Church ahead of you. Walk along the embankment and round until you reach steps which you descend to cross the road and enter the gates to St Chad's. St Chad's Well is to the left of the church behind Well Cottage. You have reached your final destination.

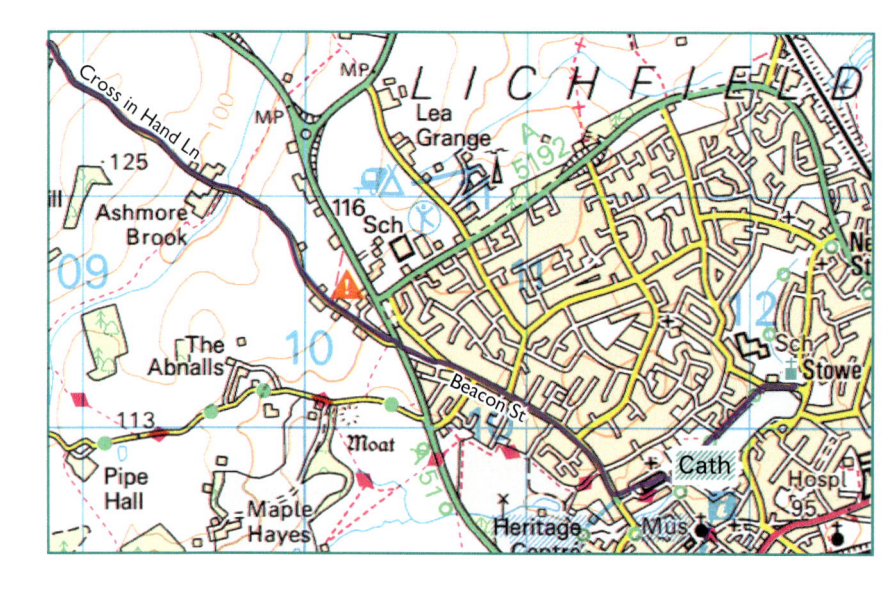

110

STAGE 16 Cannock Wood to Lichfield 5.8 miles

St Chad's Church and Well

When St Chad came to Lichfield in 669, he settled in a secluded place near a spring of water. This was where he baptised his converts. Nearby he founded a church and small monastery dedicated to St Mary. When he died in 672 he was buried nearby and the church was rededicated to him. When a cathedral was built in 700 his bones were removed there.

Nothing remains of the first Saxon church. It was rebuilt in the 12th century and parts of that structure remain. A great deal more was done in the 13th century and the church is a good example of the Early English style. Smaller changes occurred in the following centuries before a major restoration in the Victorian Gothic style in the 19th century.

St Chad's Well was a popular place of pilgrimage. In the 19th century a ten-foot-high stone structure with an arch was built with steps leading down to the well. Sadly this was demolished in 1949 and in its place the present wooden structure was built.

St Chad's Well © Paul Cox

SECTION 4 Lichfield to Stafford 20 miles

Your journey begins at St Chad's Well. You will find it to the left of the entrance to St Chad's Church behind Well Cottage. See page 111 for information about its origins. If you want to get into the pilgrim spirit you may chose to dip your finger in the well and make the sign of the cross on your forehead.

Walk out through the church gate and cross carefully over the road to ascend up to Stowe Pool and walk on the right-hand side of the pool towards the cathedral. When you leave the pool continue on down Reeve Lane to arrive at a T-junction. Turn right, then immediately left to reach the entrance to Lichfield Cathedral.

From the cathedral entrance, go ahead and at the T-junction turn right past Erasmus House and walk up Beacon Street. Continue straight ahead at the roundabout, passing Morrisons on your left.

About 250 yards after the roundabout, look out for Pinfold Road on your left and Cross in Hand Lane, which you will be following to Farewell. Further information about Cross in Hand Lane and Farewell can be found on page 108. Cross in Hand Lane is to the left of the Pinfold. This was a place where stray cattle were rounded up and kept by the 'pinner' before the enclosures. The city council still appoints two pinners and a pinlock keeper every year!

The first few yards of Cross in Hand Lane is still in the city but soon leads to the A51. You have good views here but cross with care. Cross in Hand Lane is a quintessential English lane passing through pleasant farmland. This lane is generally quiet except during the rush hour. Before you walk up the first hill look out for a small cave on the right opposite a house. Local lore has it that it was used by candle sellers in the days of medieval pilgrimage. There are a number of listed buildings along the way and in places the lane is carved out between Keuper sandstone banks. After about a mile and a half, you will pass a stream on your right called Bilson Brook. Soon after you come to Mill Farm on your left with its small lake. It is on the site of the mill that existed when there was a priory at Farewell. A few yards past Mill Farm, look out for a kissing gate on your left which you cross over and head towards the far end of St Bartholomew's Church ahead of you.

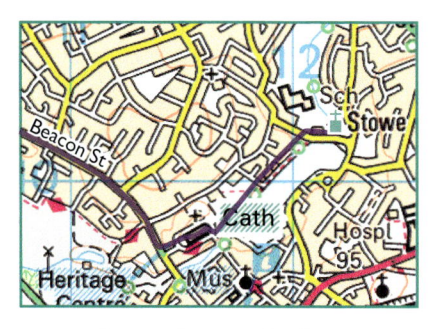

Continue on over a stream to the buildings ahead of you. Pass these on your right and continue on the footpath, following the signs across four fields, which includes passing a pond on your left. Cross over by a gate, then cross a stile on your right to go round to the right of the community hall and out onto the road where you turn left downhill. *(NB It is curious that this is the*

112

STAGE 16 Lichfield to Cannock Wood 5.8 miles

correct right of way and if the community hall gate is locked as it sometimes is, you will have to go on the more obvious path to the road ahead!) Immediately go right uphill into Ford Lane. After about 350 yards, you reach the flat x-shaped crossroads in Chorley. Go straight on into Lodge Lane, with the Malt Shovel pub on your left. After 200 yards turn left into Green Lane and then fork right into Dodd's Lane.

When you come to the end of Dodds Lane, cross straight over to a footpath called Watery Lane which leads downhill, passing Brook Farm on your left which has a statue of a deer near a pond. When you reach the bottom of Watery Lane, turn left and go uphill through woodland until you come out at a road with Windy Ridge Nursery on your left. Cross over to find a footpath along the roadside beside Gentleshaw Common. At this point we have joined the Heart of England Way. Turn right here. Just before you leave the common, turn left and over a crosspaths before taking a right turn on the next path. After 150 yards you reach the road. This dog-leg is to enable you to enjoy the good view south-west across Burntwood, but if you miss that and go ahead you will also reach the end of the common. You will then pass Christ Church and Gentleshaw Primary School on your right. You arrive at the junction of School Lane and Buds Lane. If you need the centre of Cannock Wood turn left down Buds Lane, but the Two Saints Way continues on the footpath ahead.

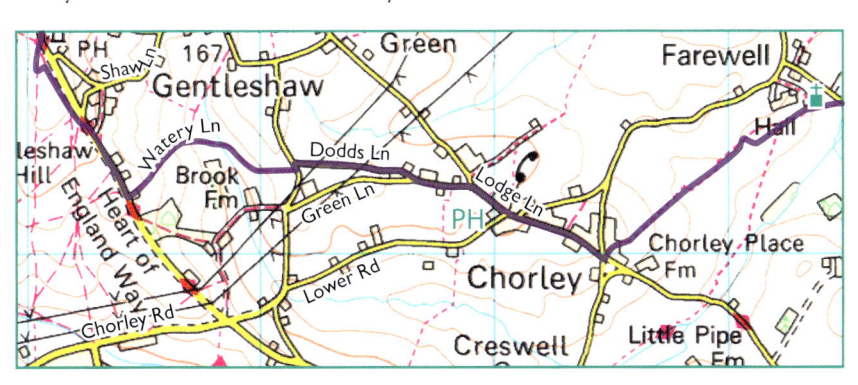

Alternative route

After very heavy rain Watery Lane may be difficult, so if this is the case, turn left at the Malt & Shovel in Chorley into Lower Road. Pass roads on your right and left continue until you come to crossroads where you turn right. Cross over to Gentleshaw Common and keep along the eastern edge and you will soon rejoin the Two Saints Way opposite Windy Ridge Nursery.

SECTION 4 Lichfield to Stafford 20 miles

Go through an avenue of trees which leads onto a tarmac lane. There is a good view back to Lichfield from here. At the end of the lane turn left, with a reservoir on your left and woodland on your right.

At the end of that path, you will see the main entrance to Beaudesert Park on your right. Beaudesert Hall, the former medieval house of the Bishops of Coventry and Lichfield, dates from 1190 and incorporates an episcopal chapel. After the Dissolution of the Monasteries in 1536, Henry VIII confiscated the Bishop's lands and gave them to Sir William Paget who became the 1st Baron of Beaudesert. Later it was constructed as an Elizabethan mansion by the 3rd Baron of Beaudesert.

Reflections Gardens, which will be of interest to pilgrims (see page 105), is down this road, but the route continues straight on along Holly Hill Road. As you bear round to the left, there is a track on your right that leads into the Beaudesert Park Scout Camp, but you may only enter if you have received prior permission (see page 104).
Next you come to the Park Gate Inn on your left which is the last pub you will pass before Stafford. Turn right here where there is a car park for Castle Ring

Woods near Castle Ring © Wendy Cleary

STAGE 15 Cannock Wood to Flaxley Green 3.2 miles

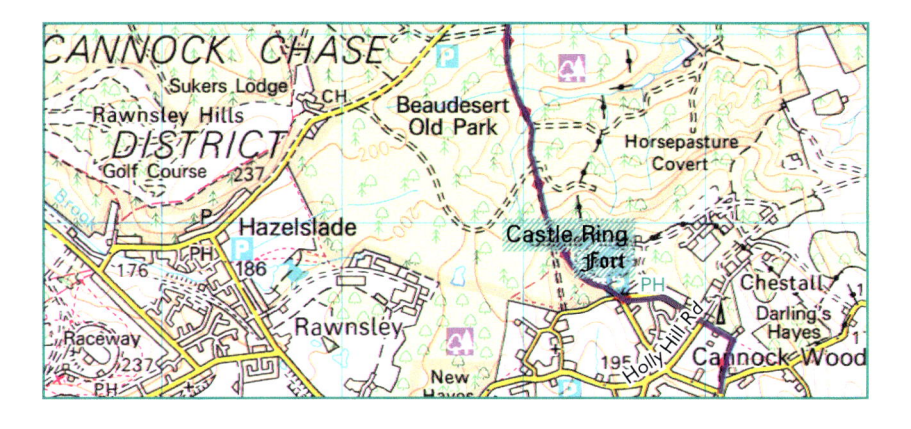

Hill Fort. See page 102 for information about this ancient fort.

Before you venture forth across Cannock Chase you may well wish to explore Castle Ring and enjoy the view, particularly to the east with Rugeley Power Station prominent. The footpath keeps to the south-west side of the hillfort and then descends through woodland to join a wider path leading quite steeply downhill to cross two fords at the bottom of the valley, the second of which has a pond to the left. This area of the Chase is called Beaudesert and in medieval times, when the Chase was called the Bishop's Chase, it was at the heart of the forest. The whole area of Cannock Chase is the remnant of what was once a huge forest in which Henry II hunted. In 1290 the hunting rights passed to the Bishops of Lichfield who hunted fallow and red deer. Cannock Chase is England's smallest Area of Outstanding Natural Beauty (AONB).

Go straight on uphill. Just before reaching a road, the footpath turns right for 400 yards before turning left to reach a crossroads. Go over into Stile Cop Road and immediately left down the track which is called Marquis Drive and which you will be following for three miles. The road is named after the Marquis of Anglesey – find out more about this colourful character on page 101.

After about half a mile, the track passes a house and a path to Miflins Valley on your right and then descends again, passing a pond on your left and a stream on your right. Just before you reach the A460 near Flaxley Green, Moors Goose Pumping Station will be on your left.

115

SECTION 4 Lichfield to Stafford 20 miles

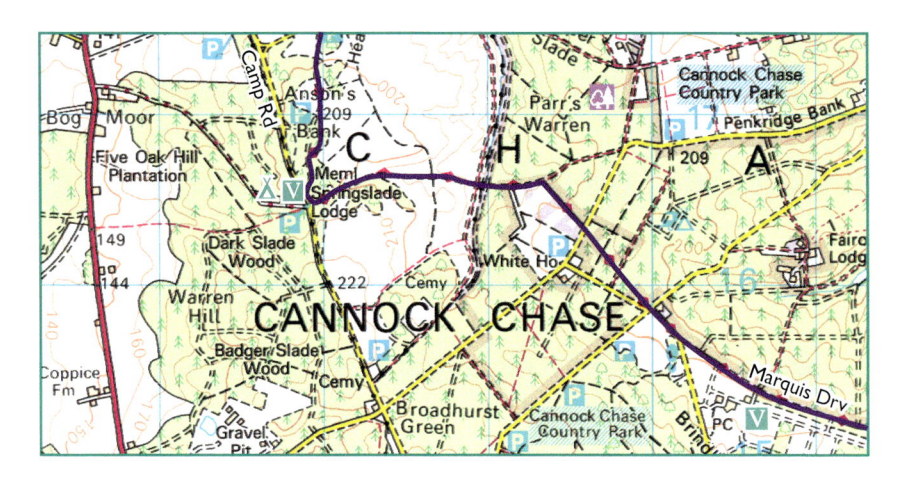

Cross carefully over the A460 and the railway and continue uphill. As you start to descend look over to the area on your left – this was called Kitbag Hill. Between here and the visitor centre half a mile ahead, a large amount of land here was occupied by RAF Hednesford and it was considered a rough deal if your quarters were up here! As the road levels out and becomes tarmac you will find an interpretation panel about RAF Hednesford on your left. Soon after, Cannock Chase Visitor Centre, with refreshments and toilets, is also on your left.

Carry straight on, passing the Burma Star Memorial Copse and an open green on your left and then you finally leave Marquis Drive, branching off to the right by a house at a crossroads. Continue along forest tracks which twice zig zag right and left to cross another road. The path soon starts to go downhill. Turn left at the next junction to go downhill and cross over the Sherbrook Valley. You now go uphill again through a stretch of open heath before entering woodland again. After passing a barrier, you will find the Katyn Memorial on your right. See page 100 for details of the poignant story behind the commemoration. A few yards further on you reach a road (Camp Road) and the Springslade Lodge tearoom, a good place to pause for refreshment, where camping is also available.

The footpath does not actually cross the road, but turns north at this point through the trees to an area of the Chase called Anson's Bank, named after the Anson family of Shugborough Hall. The most famous member of the family was Admiral George Anson who sailed round the world in 1740. His brother Thomas planted pine trees in prominent spots between here and Milford to commemorate his feat. A few yards off to your left you may

STAGE 14 Flaxley Green to Milford 6.5 miles

be able to find a toposcope which indicates highlights of the view which could at one time be appreciated from here, but now trees have obscured it.

When you come close to a road again turn right into a car park and then go left until you come to a junction of paths by a clump of birch trees where you fork left. This is a fine stretch of heathland with extensive views to the north-east. As you continue, you will now see an upland marsh pool called Womere on your left – there are very few of these in the Midlands. Local legend has it that it is bottomless, but in fact it is a shallow pond. Soon after passing Womere, the Staffordshire Way joins briefly from the west and just afterwards, also on your left, is a trig point. Behind it is a glacial boulder which stands on a plinth. This 'erratic' was carried here during the Ice Ages all the way from south-west Scotland.

Eventually you leave the open heath and it becomes more wooded. Go straight over at Freda's Grave car park at Coppice Hill. Continue uphill for a few yards to join a footpath which was formerly part of the Tackeroo Railway. This was built in 1915 to serve the training camps on the Chase during World War I. Keep on the track which bends right then left on an embankment around Mere Pits before going down a cutting. As you leave the woods, you pass a small pond on your right. Go uphill a short distance then downhill to reach the car park at Milford Common.

Stafford from Cannock Chase © Teeranlall Ramgopal

SECTION 4 Lichfield to Stafford 20 miles

From the car park, walk to the A513 and cross with care where there is a small traffic island. Continue diagonally right across the last stretch of green and turn left onto Holdiford Road. The entrance to Shugborough Hall is close by on the other side of Holdiford Road and you may well want to walk the mile or so to visit it. Cross over the railway bridge and then the bridge over the River Sow. The canal bridge that follows is humpbacked and visibility for motorists is poor, so it is advisable to approach with care and only cross when you can see and hear no traffic. Walk with care for a further 300 yards before taking the footpath on your left towards the woods.

Alternative route

If you wish to avoid negotiating the canal bridge, you may prefer to take an alternative route by going down onto the towpath of the Staffordshire and Worcestershire Canal. After 2.5 miles you will reach the bridge at Baswich Lane where you cross the road and rejoin the Two Saints Way at a stile on the north side of the road. If you take this alternative, you may also want to divert 600 yards along Baswich Lane to St Thomas Priory which you will have missed.

Before reaching the woods you come to a hedge on your left. Go off the main track here and keeping the hedge on your right you soon come to a stile (This path you are supposed to use to the south of the main track is often overgrown - you may find you have to stick to the main track through two gates here). Go ahead into the woodland and you will shortly rejoin the main track which soon reaches the end of the wood. Pass through the next small field and then another field with woodland on your left. Pass by a hill with a few pine trees and as you approach a sewage works, look for a stile which you cross to find the path which will take you round to the north of the works. The nature of your experience here may be determined by the wind direction! Eventually you will find you are corralled around to the road leading from the west to the sewage works. Walk along here for 200 yards and then branch off to the left along a pleasant green lane.

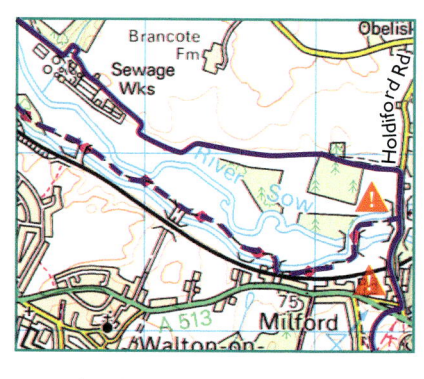

Ahead of you on your left you come to a 17th-century farmhouse called St Thomas Priory Farm. The garden includes a stretch of priory wall and a mill pond

STAGE 13 Milford to Stafford 4.6 miles

which were part of St Thomas Priory which you can find out more about on page 89. The owner Mr John Martin may be able to show you this site. Please contact him by emailing dfoss@metronet.co.uk or telephoning 01785 223 748.

Turn left into Baswich Lane (This road can be very busy and if you would like to avoid this you can use the St Thomas Lane opposite and then the new Two Waters Way as a longer but safer alternative). Some of the stones from the former priory have been used for the modern houses on your left. The road turns right then left to cross the River Sow. Soon after look out for a stile on your right just before the road crosses the canal. Cross the stile and walk over the field and cross a bridge over the River Penk.

Walk on to the next bridge which is a curiosity as it appears to have been made just to cross a fence! There now follows a pleasant stretch following the meanders of the River Sow, gradually getting closer to the sounds of Stafford ahead. When you reach a bridge, cross over the road and follow the tarmac path into Stafford which is now on the northern side of the river.

Alternative route

The section between Baswich Lane and Fairway can be subject to flooding, so if that is the case, cross straight over Baswich Lane into St Thomas Lane, then turn left into Tixall Road and follow it for two thirds of a mile, until you turn left into Dartmouth Street. At the end of the street turn left, passing the Kingston Centre on your left, then cross over at the bridge and turn right to resume the Two Saints Way.

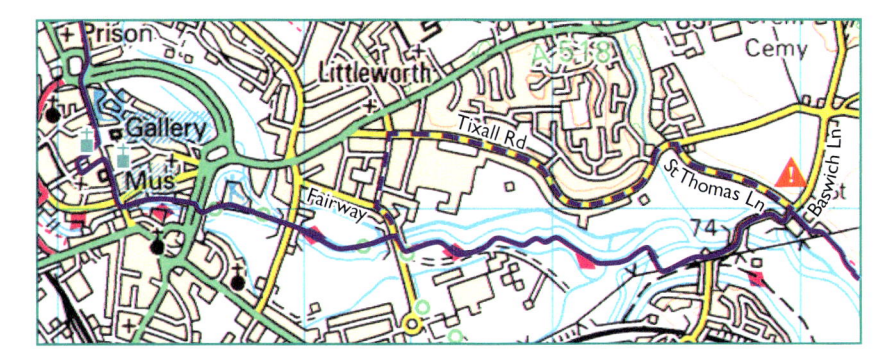

You pass an Asda superstore (the first shop since Lichfield) and after passing the council offices, turn right into Bridge Street and then across by the Nationwide Building Society into the pedestrianised Greengate Street. On your right-hand side you will soon find the church of our St Chad. Information about the church is on page 91.

SECTION 3 Stafford to Stoke 23 miles

Across from St Chad's Church, you will see the Ancient High House, England's largest timber-framed town house. Walk down the alley to the right of it and you will come to the Collegiate Church of St Mary, information about which can be found on page 89. The entrance is on the south side. After your visit, turn right and walk round the church. The outline of St Bertelin's Chapel can be seen on the western side. Return down the alley from the north side of the church and back into the pedestrianised street. Turn left and pass through the Market Square with the Shire Hall Gallery to your right.

Walk up the street which is now called Gaolgate Street and at the top, turn right. Cross over the A34 at the lights and continue into Gaol Road. After passing Stafford Prison, turn right into Crooked Bridge Road. Four hundred yards further on, cross over Corporation Street at the lights into Prospect Road. You will soon come to allotments on your right. Take the footpath through the middle of the allotments to the far end and then turn left. After passing John Street on your right, cross diagonally over a recreation ground and proceed ahead along Trenchard Avenue using the footway on the right-hand side. When you reach the end of the avenue, turn right into Portal Road. You will probably prefer to walk on the grassy area on the left-hand side. As you come to the end of that road look for a path leading out onto the busy A513. Turn right along the cycle path and footway and after crossing a stream, go on a further 200 yards before crossing the road with care. Continue up a road which will lead you past MOD buildings on your left and Staffordshire University on your right to Beacon Farm.

Pass to the right of the farm and on up the track to a kissing gate on your left. Go through this gate and across the field to the next kissing gate up the hill. Cross the farm track into another field and head uphill half left. Go through a kissing gate (this field boundary is not on all Explorer maps) and walk on to the corner of the woods ahead and circulate round to the left of Beacon Hill. There are fine views all around here of Stafford and Cannock Chase behind you. The Wrekin is 25 miles away to the west. When you have worked your way round to the northern side of the hill, take the footpath straight downhill towards the village of Hopton.

At the bottom of the hill, go across a stile and over a bridge crossing the stream and continue uphill with a hedge on your left. Cross another stile and turn left into a road with smart modern houses. Hopton has won a number of best kept village awards. At the end of this road (King's Drive) turn right up Wilmore Hill Lane. You pass a small village green

STAGE 12 Stafford to Sandon 6.3 miles

with a bench. Continue up between sandstone banks before passing the village hall on the left. At the T-junction, turn right and look for the sign pointing left to Hopton Heath Battlefield and Monument. Go through the kissing gate and take the footpath ahead of you. Just before you pass the MOD property on your right, you will find, somewhat incongruously placed behind the chain link fencing, a memorial stone and an excellent interpretation panel about the Civil War Battle of Hopton Heath, fought here on 19th March 1643.

Carry straight on, following the field boundary with the hedge on your left. You arrive at cross paths where you go straight ahead into the wood. After a few yards look for a path on the right hand side which will lead you across a stile into a large field which you cross diagonally. The path is not always well defined here. You should be able to find the path again on the far side which leads via two kissing gates across the woodland belt. Here you can enjoy a fine view of the Trent Valley with the village of Salt below and the Sandon Hall estate on the hill behind. You will be following the valley for about 20 miles.

Go straight down the hill to a kissing gate. The footpath goes straight across the field, but if the farmer has not kept it open, you may need to make a short diversion to the right and left around the crop. The path leads you into Salt, where you turn right and soon pass the attractive thatched Hollybush Inn on your right. For more information about Salt turn to page 86. Take the next road on your left. This leads across the River Trent. You will pass two seats on the right-hand side giving you a choice of views either east or west. To the east in Sandon Park is an urn-topped column commemorating William Pitt, which was erected in 1806. When you reach the Trent & Mersey Canal, go down the steps and turn left to head north along the towpath. For more information about the history of the canal, turn to page 58.

When you reach bridge no. 83 on the B5066, the Dog & Doublet pub at Sandon is 150 yards to the right.

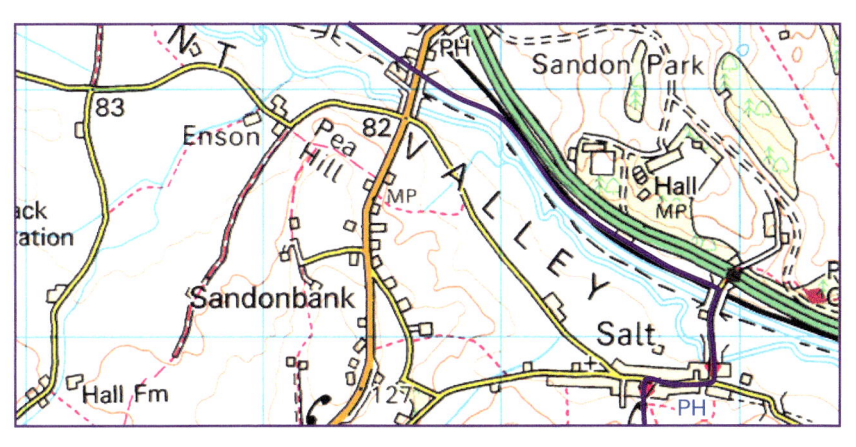

SECTION 3 Stafford to Stoke 23 miles

Continue along the canal passing under bridge no. 84. When you reach the next bridge (no. 85) you turn off to cross the bridge, but before you leave the bridge, take a look ahead at the field on the eastern side of the canal, where a clump of trees hides a well, known as St Rufin's or St Chad's Well. Hereabouts also was a chapel dedicated to St Rufin's, no doubt often visited by pilgrims in the Middle Ages. To find out more about the Legend of St Wulfad and St Rufin, turn to page 78. It is thought that the last stones were probably cleared and used in the construction of the canal in the 1770s. Walk on along the lane which will bring you out to the delightful village of Burston.

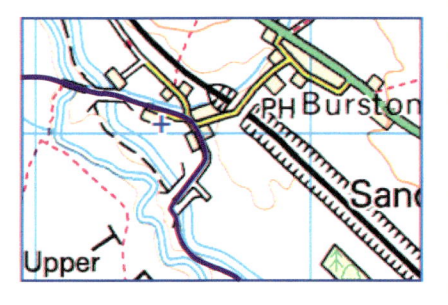

St Rufin's Well © David Pott

Turn left, passing a small car park. On the right is a millpond and on the left an attractive row of cottages. St Rufin's Church, tucked behind the first cottage, is a very unassuming building which blends inconspicuously into the scene. It was built in 1859 and replaced an older chapel. It is often open, but if not, the key should be available at cottage no. 9.

Continue past the cottages and the millpond and take the footpath ahead beside a stream that leads you to a bridge over the canal. Continue ahead to cross a metal bridge over the River Trent. You now enter a nature reserve with a lake on your right. Go over a stile and then straight ahead and cross over two large fields, until you reach a lane leading to the village of Aston.

Turn right here up Aston Lane. The lane bears right and when it ends you carry on along a pleasant path which skirts around Aston Hall. You come out onto a road with the entrance back into Aston Hall on your left. To find out more about the history of the hall, turn to page 83. To see if it is possible to visit the beautiful chapel at Aston Hall, where the bones of St Chad were

122

STAGE 11 Sandon to Stone 4.9 miles

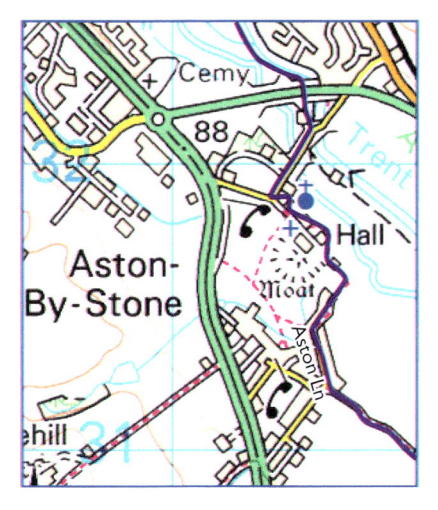

found in 1839, please ring Deacon Trevor beforehand on 01785 812 001 or email him on deacontrevor@hotmail.co.uk. Go right, through St Saviour's churchyard and then turn right into a road which leads you over the River Trent. When you reach the canal, turn right to gain access to the towpath where you turn left and go under the bridge. After passing under the busy A51, walk a further mile into Stone.

When you arrive at the centre of Stone at bridge no. 93, turn off the canal and turn right to cross the canal and continue ahead past the Swan Inn on your right and cross Abbey Street to reach Earl St Vincent Square, so named after Stone's famous son Admiral John Jervis, a colleague of Lord Nelson who became Earl St Vincent after defeating the Spanish off Cape St Vincent in 1797. Turn right into Lichfield Street.

Cross Lichfield Street with care and turn right. Soon on your left is Priory House. In the basement of the house, which is privately owned, is a vaulted crypt from the Augustinian Priory and in the garden there are a few more ruins. These are the oldest parts of Stone. It may be possible to see these by arrangement with the owner, Timothy Gillow by phoning him on 01785 818 688 or e-mail him on thegillows@yahoo.co.uk.

Walk a few yards up Lichfield Street, take the path up to St Michael & St Wulfad's Church and walk round left and right to the front of the church. If the church is not open or if you wish to make arrangements to visit before you arrive please contact Dennis Abbott on 01785 814 134 or e-mail dennis.abbott@gmail.com. For more information about the church and former priory, turn to page 80

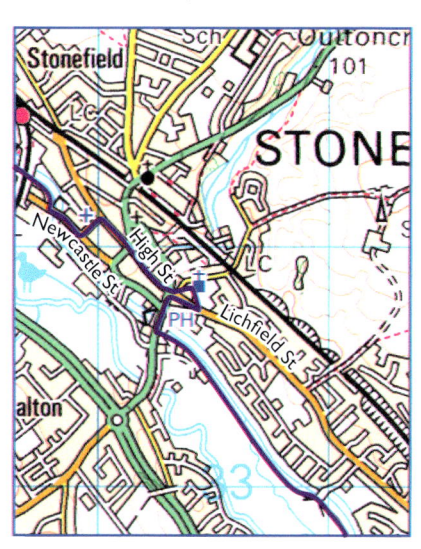

123

SECTION 3 Stafford to Stoke 23 miles

From the front of the church, walk down the path ahead of you and turn left into Church Street, then right into Lichfield Street. Cross over at the lights into the pedestrianised High Street. You pass Cumberland House on your left where the Duke of Cumberland stayed when the Redcoat army were stationed here during the Jacobite Rebellion of 1745. Walk up the High Street, passing the Crown Hotel also on your left. This was once an important staging post for coaches travelling between London and Scotland.

At the top of the High Street you will see some railings about the legend of Wulfad and Rufin which is the foundational story of Stone. Cross over at the lights into Station Road, passing the thatched Granville's pub on your left and Wetherspoons in the former post office on the right. Turn left into Margaret Street and cross over to visit St Dominic's Catholic Church which has a stonework relief depicting the legend of Wulfad and Rufin. If the church is closed you may find that one of the sisters at the convent is able to show you round. Phone 01785 812 091 if you wish to check in advance. Turn to page 77 to find out more about the life of Dominic Barberi.

Turn right into Newcastle Street and you will soon reach the canal again where you cross the bridge and turn right to continue northwards past the lock along the towpath. Continue for another mile until you reach the Meaford Flight of locks which ascends over 30 feet. Here, at bridge no. 97, you leave the canal and turn left into a field. Follow the path down to a road where you turn left and after 40 yards turn right into Meadow View. As you approach the A34, you pass the George & Dragon on your left. Walk on a further 50 yards and cross the busy A34 with care.

Keep on the left hand side, crossing the River Trent and passing a garage and then continue uphill on the A51. After a third of a mile you pass a farm on your right and shortly you will need to cross carefully over the A51 to a stile and across the small field to the next stile. Turn right here and follow the farm track round to the left. The wooded hill, which has been on your right since the roundabout, is Bury Bank. There is an ancient hill fort here which still has quite impressive ramparts though they are well covered in bracken. It is strange to think that for a short time this was probably the capital of the ancient kingdom of

STAGE 10 Stone to Tittensor 4.9 miles

Mercia. The former name for it was Wulpherecestre – Wulphere's camp. This hill fort was located at a very significant junction as it was where travellers going north either journeyed north-west for Chester, North Wales and Ireland, or north to Scotland.

The track leads downhill then uphill to a stile into Forestry Commission land. This lane is sometimes called Nuns Walk, possibly because at some time nuns were living in Bury Bank House on the other side of A51 which you have just crossed. After crossing the stile notice on your right a prominent mound in the field. This is called Saxon's Lowe. This mound possibly dates from the Iron Age period, in which case why is it called Saxon's Lowe? One possibility is that because it already had associations as a significant burial place, it was chosen by King Wulphere, the Saxon King of Mercia as his special place of burial. He died in AD 675.

Continue across Tittensor Chase where there has been storm damage. At one particular point there is a good view across the Trent Valley to Barlaston Hall and soon after there is pleasant parkland on your right, belonging to the Copeland family who made their money in the pottery industry. The path leads to a road which you cross over and go on ahead. Continue downhill, with fields on your left and Cumberstone Wood on your right. When you reach the road, turn right. Continue down the road and after passing Groundslow Farm on your left, look out for the footpath on your right. Before you take the path, you may like to go and have a look at the rich variety of ornamental ducks on the lake a few yards to your left on Beechdale Road.

Carry on for 500 yards with reservoir ponds to your left. Take the next path on your left, passing the reservoir and going uphill through the woods until you reach a path leading between houses into Tittensor, information about which can be found on page 74. Go right and left into Bracken Close. On your right you soon come to St Luke's, Tittensor with its distinctive timber-framed tower. The church is usually open.

When you leave the church, turn right along Copeland Avenue and at the T-junction turn right into Winghouse Lane, just after the post office and village store.

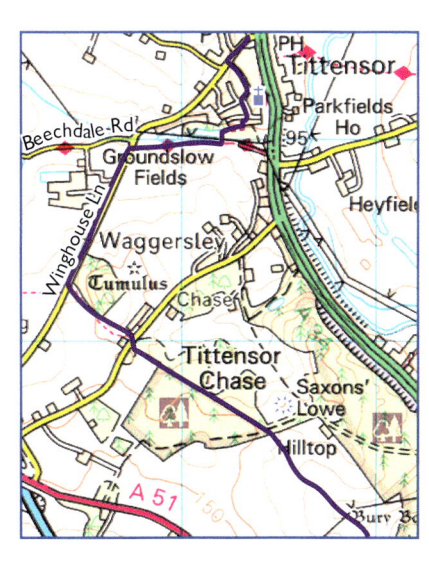

SECTION 3 Stafford to Stoke 23 miles

Take the second road on your left, Monument Lane, passing some attractive cottages on your right. Where Monument Lane bears left, go straight ahead along the track into the Trentham Estate. After 300 yards, you will find a gate on your left and when you go through it there are a number of tracks through the woods which lead up to the monument. The Two Saints Way goes right up a spur with some evidence of quarrying in the past on your left. If you prefer a slightly longer and less steep alternative follow the Monument Walk to the left. You will eventually find your way up to be confronted by the huge statue of the Duke of Sutherland – he has a very commanding view! Trentham Lake is in the foreground with the Italian Gardens at the far end. Stoke spreads back into the valleys and hills beyond. Mow Cop with its folly is due north and to the northeast is the Peak District. Turn to page 69 for details about the history of Trentham.

From the monument if you are facing the view, take the track that leads off to the left via a gate and stile. It heads round in a northwesterly direction. A main path leads downhill, but you keep on the higher ground. You will come to a gate which you pass through and enter a field. Follow the track uphill and pause at the top to enjoy the view to the east across the Trent Valley. Barlaston Hall is directly opposite. It was built in 1756 and eventually bought by the most famous pottery family – the Wedgwoods. Below to the left is the Wedgwood Visitor Centre and factory.

The path follows a fence on your left then goes steeply down to a stream and then steeply up again. The high fence of the Trentham Monkey Forest is on your right. Some of the Barbary macaques that live here roost overnight at this end, so you are unlikely to see them unless you pass by early morning or late evening. For the next two thirds of a mile, you walk through King's Wood. You may prefer to use a parallel path 10 to 15 yards to the right of the main path which is also drier after wet weather. Keep a lookout for the black fallow deer which are frequently seen here. To your left are fields leading down to a lake and the M6 motorway. When you come to a high fence, go through the gateway and straight ahead into an area known as Seven Sisters. Some suppose this is because you may count seven hillocks along the ridge, but it was more likely named after a stand of beech trees.

Between the path and the M6 below is an attractive heathland area which is a rare and threatened habitat in the Midlands.

You descend steeply off the ridge and when you reach the bottom beside the motorway, turn right down an attractive path through the woods which was once a main driveway to Trentham Hall. After passing through two wooden gates, you come close to a high fence on your right and you bear left here and walk on to pass through a kissing gate. Cross a bridge, turn right and after 100 yards, you will find St Mary's, Trentham on your right.

Information about the church can be found on page 70.

STAGE 9 Tittensor to Stoke Minster 6.8 miles

From the church, turn right, cross the river and turn right with a car park on your left before crossing the bridge over the River Trent. When you reach the A34, go across at the pedestrian lights, turn right and walk 200 yards towards the roundabout.

Shortly before you reach the roundabout, you will find on your left the entry to

Alternative route

You may well wish to divert to Trentham Gardens and Shopping Village. From the church, if the gate is open immediately on your right, go into it and pass the courtyard on your right. Continue through another gate and over the River Trent and follow the path round to the garden centre and shops. To rejoin the Two Saints Way, go out to the A34 and cross over at the pedestrian lights, then turn left and you will soon rejoin the route on your right into Longton Brook.

a footway along the pleasant Longton Brook. It is alive with birdsong and flowers in spring, including a powerful smelling patch of wild garlic. The path crosses a road and then arrives at a second road (New Inn Lane). Turn left here and after passing St Werburgh's Drive on your left, turn right into Pacific Road. After a few yards you can resume your way by Longton Brook on your left. Carry on over one road (Omega Road) and the path goes behind houses with the brook on your left. After 200 yards, turn right between the houses and cross Constance Road and straight into Winnipeg Close. Turn left into Michigan Grove at the end of which is a short connecting footpath which leads into Pacific Road. Turn left here and after 100 yards, turn right into Atlantic Grove. At the end of this cul-de-sac you will find a ramp that leads up to the canal towpath and you resume your journey north.

Continue onwards for a mile, passing through open countryside until you arrive in Stoke with the huge incinerator on your left and the Britannia Stadium, the home of Stoke City Football Club, on your right. Pass under the A50. Where the canal crosses the infant River Trent, you pass a boatyard which curiously also offers fishing, shooting and line dancing! When you reach bridge no. 112, leave the canal. Turn left and cross over the traffic lights at the slip road off the A500. Cross again at the lights to the northern side of Church Street and turn left. Enter the churchyard of Stoke Minster on your right and pass the tomb of Josiah Wedgwood, which is in front of the 13th century arches, sometimes locally referred to as the MacDonald Arches! Carry on under the arches and look out for the Saxon preaching cross to your left before coming to the entrance to the minster. For information about the Minster, see page 65.

SECTION 2 Stoke to Nantwich 24 miles

When you leave the Minster, the one-way street in front of you is Glebe Street. Turn right and keep on the pavement as it bends to the left and then right to cross over the A500. Descend to the canal and resume your northward journey. You will pass Hanley Cemetery on the opposite bank and soon afterwards you will see two bottle ovens on the left. These are part of the Lock 38 development which is sited on the place of the invention of the flushing toilet. A new ideal 'model' factory, Cliffe Vale Pottery, was built here by T. W. Twyford in 1887, and his factory manufactured the world's first flushing toilets and other innovative sanitaryware for over 100 years, changing the way billions of people lived around the world. The Twyfords works closed in 1994 and moved to a purpose-built factory at Alsager. After passing the impressive flight of Stoke Locks, you arrive at Etruria, the point of junction between the Trent & Mersey Canal and the Caldon Canal.

You turn sharp right here over a bridge and pass the Etruria Industrial Museum on your right (see page 64). Etruria was named after a district in Italy where the Etruscans developed designs which were a major inspiration for the great potter Josiah Wedgwood. He established his works here in 1769 and they remained in operation until 1950 when the factory moved a few miles south to Barlaston.

Continue by the green to follow the towpath along the Caldon Canal (see page 63) and proceed up the staircase locks at Bedford Street. The canal winds its way until it come out into Hanley Park which was landscaped by Thomas Mawson and opened in 1897. You leave the canal on reaching an ornamental bridge. Cross over to the northern side and go left of the bandstand. Follow the path, keeping the playground to your left and exit the park into Regent Street. Cross over the road and you will soon pass the City Central Mosque on your left. You would be welcome to visit and if the mosque is closed, phone Rana M Tufail on 01782 610 548 and he may be available to open up and show you round.

Take the next road on your left (Hinde Street) which soon bears round to the right to reach Potteries Way. Cross over at the pedestrian lights where the building ahead of you with the bottle oven was formerly Smithfield Pottery. Turn right and immediately left into Warner Street. When you come soon to a small park on your right, cross diagonally up to Bethesda Street and turn left to visit the Potteries Museum immediately on your left. Information about the museum and the wonderful Anglo-Saxon Hoard which is exhibited here can be found on page 62. For a history of The Potteries, see page 57.

Turn left out of the museum, crossover at the lights and then go left down Broad Street before turning right into the pedestrian access before the Mitchell Arts Centre. Walk round with Tesco on your left. This is surprisingly the only shop that is directly on your route between Tittensor and Chesterton! When you reach The Potteries Way again, turn right and then cross over at the lights to carry

STAGE 8 Stoke Minster to Bradwell 7.8 miles

on downhill past the car sales on your left. Turn left into Etruria Road and on towards the flyover which you will cross under by turning left and immediately right at the pedestrian lights. Turn right and notice on your left the J. Arthur Rank gong man on what was the entrance sign for the Festival Garden. Continue ahead, crossing over Marina Way with the roundabout with the swan sculpture to your right. Go ahead and on your left you will pass a colossal head of Josiah Wedgwood made from large bricks. The building on the left of the Moat House Hotel complex, set back on your left across the grass, is the Etruria Hall where Josiah Wedgwood once lived. At this point cross over the road and take the footpath opposite where there is a notice about access to Festival Park.

This path leads up into Festival Park where the National Garden Festival was held in 1986. It is an intriguing area where various objects left over from the festival can still be discovered. You start by forking right then walking left up a Welsh slate path where there was once a waterfall. Continue up hill bearing left, then up flights of steps to find a circular grass patch. Descend here on the straight path ahead. You will pass a sculpture on your right called 'Windborne – the Phoenix' by Keir Smith before you arrive at a stone circle.

At the stone circle, turn right and after about 20 yards take the next path on the left off the wider one. You pass two sets of steps on your left before coming out by a stand of eucalyptus in a wood and stone circle. Pass to the left of them and half left

up a path, passing more eucalyptus on your left. When you come to a fence on your left, the path bears right to a circular amphitheatre which includes stones at the four main compass points. Continue straight ahead on the opposite side of the circle. Soon after passing a standing stone on your left, you come to a bridge over a small ravine. This bridge is now closed, so walk down on the right and then up the opposite bank to rejoin the path. Go ahead to a clump of fir trees. Turn right here and after 120 yards you will find a low wooden palisade which you pass on your left.

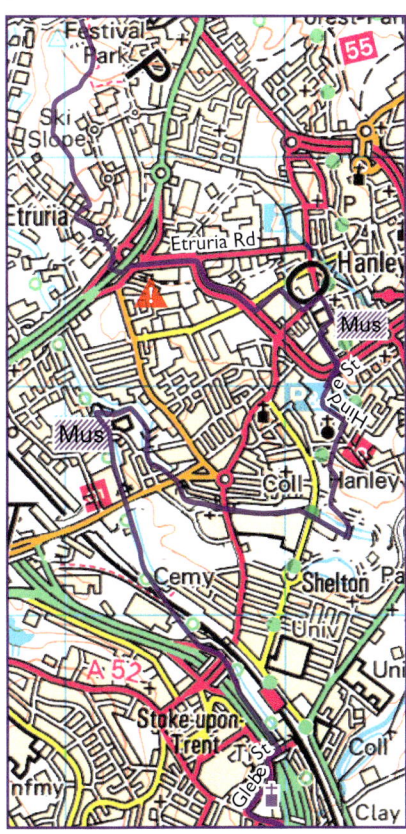

SECTION 2 Stoke to Nantwich 24 miles

Here you come out on a tarmac path where you turn left and then fork half right to ascend to the top of the hill where there is a good view across the retail park to Hanley. Go down on a path between trees with allotments to your right. Pass over a rise between some palm trees and continue straight ahead to the tarmac path. Pass a cricket ground on your right and a barrier with the Grange Park Greenway sign. In medieval times there was a Grange Farm here which supplied food for the monks at Hulton Abbey which is now called Abbey Hulton!

Continue straight ahead, passing a playground on your left. At the cross paths, go down the flight of steps and continue ahead, passing a pond on your right. Turn off the path onto a smaller track to pass some allotments on your left. Turn left so that the allotments are on your left and houses on your right. Turn right and when you reach the corner of the housing estate, go diagonally right across a field. Leave the field crossing straight over the access track to a scrap dealers on your left. This was once the main warehouse for the Burslem Arm stretch of canal.

Take the narrow path ahead, crossing an old canal bridge and going straight up to the road and new housing development ahead. Turn left taking the wide path behind the new apartment complex. Walk to the end, noting the sign marking the site of the former Burslem Port. Turn right along the side of the apartments, which is Luke Street. Turn left onto Newport Lane. Just before you reach the canal on your right is Oliver's Mill, built in 1909. It includes two calcining ovens, one in the traditional bottle shape and the other one square with a heavily moulded cap. At the bridge here (no 123), go down to the canal and turn left to resume your journey northwards.

The names in this area – Newport, Middleport, Westport and Longport – allude to the wharfingering communities that once existed here which were involved in handling the import and export of cargoes to The Potteries. When you reach bridge 125, you may well well want to cross over and turn left and walk the 250 yards to Middleport Pottery which has an excellent visitor centre and café. See **middleportpottery.co.uk** After resuming your journey, you pass under the busy A527 (bridge no. 126), there is a fine bottle kiln on the opposite side of the canal. About 100 yards further on, take a footpath to the left between a mill building and woodland.

This is the significant point on the pilgrimage where the predominantly northerly direction of the route becomes predominantly westerly.

However, before you continue you may wish to walk a few yards up the canal to Westport Lake where there is a visitor centre with good facilities and refreshments available.

STAGE 8 Stoke Minster to Bradwell 7.8 miles

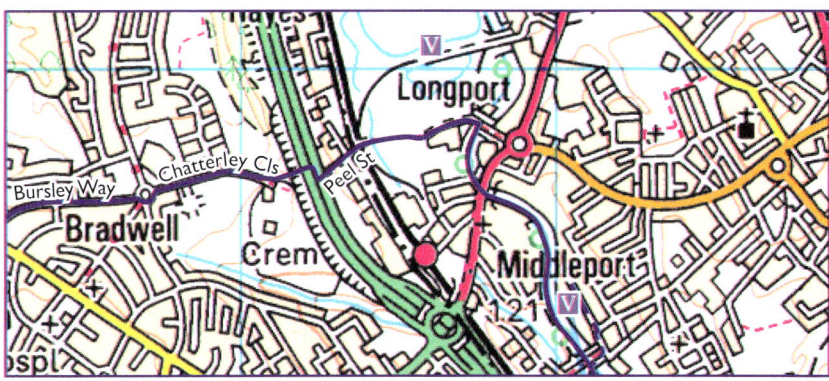

Middleport Pottery © David Haden

Take the path which leads down to the railway line, passing a big boulder on your left en route. Cross over the railway line, carry straight on up Peel Street and as you approach the A500 find a path on the right which leads to an underpass. On the other side are steps going steeply up through woodland. You will come out onto a road (Chatterley Close) where you go straight ahead to a roundabout.

Continue on into Bursley Way, passing a school on your right. At the end of that road, turn right into Bradwell Lane which soon leads you to the busy A34.

131

SECTION 2 Stoke to Nantwich 24 miles

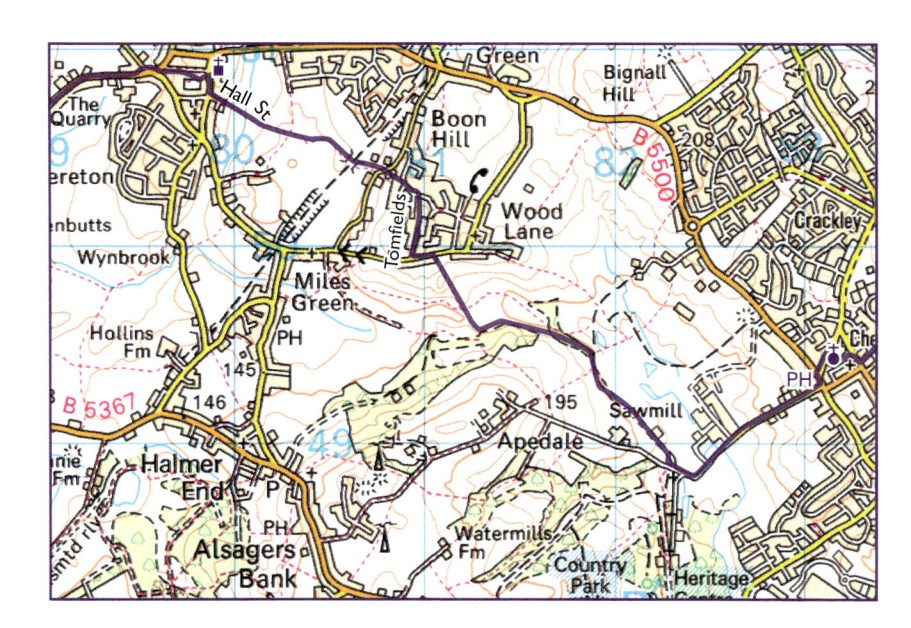

Cross over at the lights, turn right and take the footpath on the left which leads up to the top of a park. Go through the park and down the hill to find the exit left into Brick Kiln Lane. When you reach the main road, turn right and then go up the path through the churchyard to Holy Trinity Church, Chesterton, information about which can be found on page 55.

From the front of the church, go to the road and turn left, pass the Red Lion Pub on your left, at the end of Church street turn left, cross the road and then turn right into Apedale road. Go down this road, which bends to the right at the bottom of the hill. After passing the entrance to Thorp Precast (marked as a sawmill on some maps), take the footpath on your right along the Newcastle Way. At this point your urban pilgrimage is over and you are in the Apedale Country Park, information about which can be found on page 54.

STAGE 7 Bradwell to Audley 3.5 miles

As you continue, Burley Farm is on your left. The route at this point is along a disused railway line. Go ahead at the green barrier and after a further half mile, you turn right to cross an area that is often frequented by bikers. Continue straight across the valley bottom and on uphill until you come out onto a road opposite Wood Lane Primary School. Turn left here and then right up Tomfields. Continue ahead on a footpath past a children's play area and field on your right. This leads to a road where you turn left. Pass two roads on your left and then take a footpath on your left (between houses) which descends between holly bushes and is known as 'Narrow Nick'.

When you exit onto a road turn left and right down another narrow path and cross over a paddock to reach a disused railway which you go over. Cross a small field and then turn right. Skirt round a damp patch and go through to the next field where you turn immediately left and walk into a lane which is often muddy. Pass a gate on your left and then cross a stile also on your left. Go right over another a damp patch and then uphill passing between two trees and then walking half right after a fence post. At the corner of the field, go through the hedge across a duck board into a field and go down the hill with the hedge on your right to reach a kissing gate where you go through to Leddy's Field Wildlife area. Cross a bridge with a pond to the right and go up the steps, leaving the reserve through attractive railings. You will soon pass Audley Theatre on your right. Turn right and you will shortly arrive at St James' Church.

SECTION 2 Stoke to Nantwich 24 miles

Cross the road ahead and walk towards the Butchers Arms. After passing the pub you will find a shady path on your left which you should take. It will lead down to a road where you turn right and immediately left to walk out of the village. After passing a garage on your left and Audley Cricket ground on your right, look for the footpath on your right and ascend Kent Hills. As you reach the top, pause to enjoy the view behind you of Audley with the Wedgwood Monument prominent on the hill behind it. Mow Cop with its folly is to the north-east. Make your way through kissing gates to the other side of the hill where you see the Cheshire Plain with the Welsh hills in the distance. There is an underground reservoir to your left. Carry on down the hill, keeping to the left hand field boundary. When you come out onto a road, turn left and when you reach a crossroads by New Peel Farm, turn right.

This road soon leads you across the M6. Walk about 250 yards further then take a footpath left across a field which soon descends into a valley by some houses. Go straight ahead on the gravel road. The next half mile along the wooded valley of Dean Brook is arguably one of the prettiest stretches on the Two Saints Way.
The steep banks are well endowed with flowers in spring and the valley floor is varied with small fields, damns and bridges. Just before you arrive at Mill Dale Farm, look out for the path which doubles back up out of the valley to come out over a stile into a large field.

Cross over this field diagonally to the left of the tree ahead. This is a permissive route. As you get closer to the field boundary look for the next footpath sign which will lead you over a stile and down some steps. Go ahead with a hedge on your right and then straight on over the next field. Cross over the next field and the stile is about 50 yards to the left of a gate. In the next field keep a pond to your right and go towards the trees which sometimes screen Barthomley Church behind them. Historical details about this church can be found on *page 52*. You come to a stile which you cross over, turn right and cross another stile to go left past a small pond and out by the church. *(NB Some field boundaries in this section indicated on the Explorer map are not there any more.)*

After visiting the church, the route turns left, but you may wish to turn right for a few yards to enjoy the thatched and timber-framed buildings, including the White Lion Inn, which was built in 1614 and is one of the finest pubs in the country. Going west out of the village you pass another fine timber-framed house, Old Hall Farm, on your right. Continue along the road until you arrive at Englesea Brook. Turn left to find Englesea Brook Primitive Methodist Chapel and Museum on your left and the cemetery on your right. Turn to *page 51* for information about the chapel and museum.

STAGE 6 Audley to Hough 7.3 miles

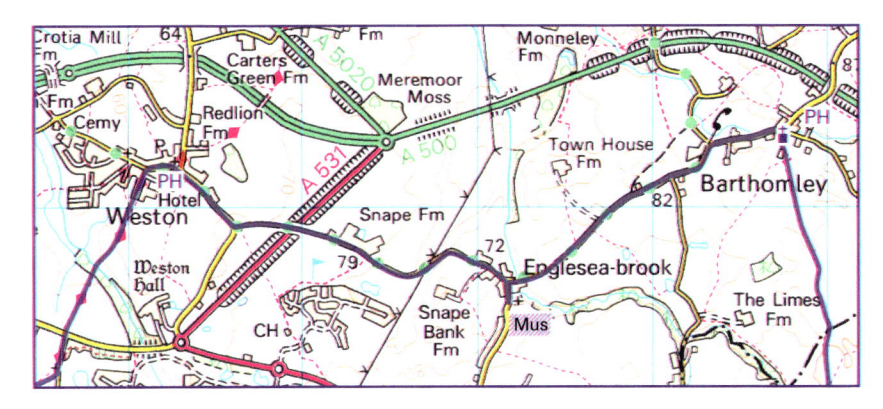

Return from the chapel back to the junction and turn left up Snape Lane. You walk over the hill and cross a valley before going gently uphill again, passing Snape Farm on your right. Cross over the A531 and at the next junction bear right to the village of Weston. Turn left when you reach the village with the White Lion pub on your left and the small Anglican red brick church on your right. At this point the Two Saints Way joins the Crewe & Nantwich Circular Walk, so look out for the black and white crossed swords waymarks.

After passing the shop, take the next road (East Avenue) on your left. At the end of that road, go through the kissing gate and soon cross a stile across a field corner to go through a strip of woodland. Cross another field and another slightly larger strip of woodland. After crossing the next field, you reach a road which you go over into Chorlton Lane.

Turn right onto a footpath immediately after the Methodist chapel. Go over stiles and past stables to cross the bridge over the railway. As you continue, there are ponds in the field to your left. The path keeps to the right of the hedges, but there is a permissive path on the other side of the hedge that might sometimes prove a drier alternative. The path crosses a farm track and stiles. This section can be very muddy but there are some helpful duck boards where it is most wet. Cross another stile into a reedy willow woodland crossing two bridges before going over a stile into a field.

Continue ahead, keeping a tree-fringed pond on your right and the oak trees to your left and make for the corner of the field. You will find a lane here with holly bushes on your left and high fencing on your right. Proceed through a kissing gate and the path bears left with woodland and then a football field on your left. You have now reached Hough.

135

SECTION 2 Stoke to Nantwich 24 miles

Turn left and as you reach the end of the football field, look out for a path on your right. Cross over two stiles into a damp meadow and then through a kissing gate just before Dove House Farm. Here you turn right. Proceed through more kissing gates across two fields, keeping to the right hand field boundary. Over to your left you will see Wybunbury Tower. You will walk a wide half circle to reach it over the next mile. When you reach the third much larger field, continue until you reach a kissing gate in the wood on your right. Do not go through this, but turn left here, crossing the field to a fishpond by Cockshades Farm. At the end of the pond, cross over and head down diagonally across some paddocks.

Go straight ahead here, leaving the Crewe & Nantwich Circular Walk temporarily, to cross over the eastern end of Wybunbury Moss National Nature Reserve. If you have time, you might like to explore the reserve and return here. This is a very special wildlife area. The Moss lies within a hollow left at the end of the last ice age, but salt subsidence has since played a part. Rare plants that live in this unusual, but dangerous mossland habitat include sundew, bog asphodel and bog rosemary. During the summer, look out for colourful dragonflies hunting along the pathways.

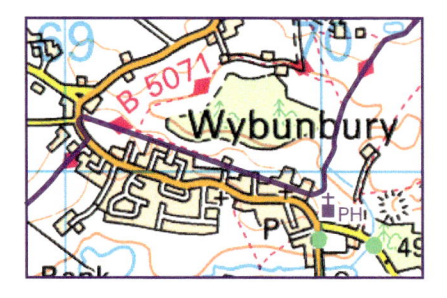

Go straight up the hill to arrive at St Chad's Tower (also called Wybunbury Tower). See page 48 for background information. Turn right out of the churchyard, passing the Swan Inn on your right. Unless you want to call first at the village shop, take the first right turn into Kiln Lane. Cross the stile by a gate and turn left. Go ahead, crossing two more stiles and over a driveway with a house on your right. This leads to a shaded path and then through a gate. Continue along the narrow field with houses on your left and Wybunbury Moss below to the right. Carry on across further stiles, rejoining the Crewe & Nantwich Circular Walk, until you reach the road where you turn left and after 80 yards turn right down an attractive lane between two houses.

After 500 yards, look for a gate with a stile to your right. Cross over the stile and walk over a field with some small ponds. When you reach the road, turn right and soon after passing the entrance to Yew Tree Farm, take the path on your left which soon crosses the farm lane.

STAGE 5 Hough to Nantwich 6.4 miles

Go on to the field boundary ahead and look for an old tree stump where you go through a gap and then ahead now keeping the field boundary on your right. After 300 yards turn right and proceed over stiles crossing three fields until you reach Stapeley Hall. Here you turn left and soon reach the A51.

Cross with care here into First Dig Lane. After a third of a mile you reach the A529, where you turn right and after 200 yards look for the footpath on your left. Cross over two stiles and over a small field to another stile by a pond. Cross diagonally to the far right hand corner to locate the next stile to the next field which you cross to reach a road. Turn left to Mill Bank Farm. As you enter the farm, the road turns to the right and soon after you take the footpath to the left which crosses over a bridge. The path swings left to cross another bridge and then goes up a hill. This is a permissive path. As you reach the top of the hill turn right and cross the stile into a field. Continue straight ahead with fencing on your left and over the next stile. Cross straight over the field and after crossing another stile go half right across a small field to reach a track. Turn left here passing stables on your left. The track leads out via a kissing gate to a road where you go straight ahead soon passing Church House Farm on your right.

When you reach the A530, turn right and cross over the bridge. Cross over the A530 here and pick up a path which will take you alongside the River Weaver on your left, with a park and lakes on your right. Eventually you will pass under a railway bridge. Soon after cross over to the other side of the river and turn immediately right. After 400 yards, turn right to cross the Mill Bridge. Cross over the road and into Mill Street which leads you into Nantwich High Street. Turn left here and on your right is the Queen's Aid House. This was built after The Great Fire of 1583 which lasted for 20 days and destroyed most of the town. There is a plaque commemorating the grattitude of the town to Queen Elizabeth I for her help in raising funds to rebuild the town. You will soon reach the town square where you turn right to St Mary's Church which is your destination. You'll find further details about the church on page 43.

SECTION 1 Nantwich to Chester 22.5 miles

After you have visited the church return to the High Street and turn right. At the end of the High Street, turn left and cross over the A534 and Town Bridge into the attractive Welsh Row with several fine timber-framed houses, including Sir Roger Wilbraham's almshouses and Malthouse Cottage (now the Cheshire Cat). As you walk on, you have a good view of the canal viaduct ahead of you as you pass Mallbank School and Sixth Form College on your right. Cross over the lights and take the slip path up to the Shropshire Union Canal. (see page 33 for information about the Shropshire Union Canal). Pass the wooden statue of a dog on your right and continue ahead. This is an important location as it marks the end of the old Chester Canal, completed in 1794, and the beginning of the Birmingham & Liverpool Junction Canal, which was constructed in 1834 and which carries on south to Wolverhampton. When you reach Acton Bridge (no. 93), leave the canal and cross it, pausing to look at the interpretation board about the Civil War Battle of Nantwich which took place here. When you arrive at the village, turn right (Wilbraham Road) and then cross over the A534 to St Mary's Church which is a few yards to your left. Turn to page 42 for some information about the church.

Alternative route

If it is very wet or you are short of time you may wish to walk west from the church along Monks Lane and straight on along the A534 until you reach the canal at Burland where you turn right and rejoin the main route.

Monks Lane is so called because monks from Combermere Abbey used to take services in Acton. There is a pavement all the way, but you would miss out on walking through some attractive landscapes.

After visiting the church, turn right, passing the Star pub on your right and as the main road starts to bear left, go straight ahead. Soon after, at a junction of footpaths, turn right and walk across three fields. Cross over a stile to follow an attractive line of birch trees on your left as you skirt Madam's Farm. This leads onto an unmade road where you continue ahead to cross a minor road. Go on ahead, crossing two more fields to the corner of Long Plantation.

Cross the stile and go diagonally right to exit left onto a road (Swanley Lane). After 100 yards, cross a road on your left and descend to the Llangollen Canal and turn right under the bridge. Information about the Llangollen Canal can be found on page 40.

You will soon pass Swanley Lock and Swanley Marina and there follows a quiet and attractive two mile stretch to Hurleston Junction.

STAGE 4 Nantwich to Barbridge 6 miles

Alternative route

When you reach bridge no. 4, you may well choose to make a diversion to Snugburys famous Jersey ice cream which you can reach by following the white posts across the fields for half a mile to Park Farm. Snugburys is also famous for the huge straw sculptures that are made each year. After your visit, walk north keeping on the left hand side for quarter of a mile up the A51 and rejoin the canal at the bridge there.

The highlight of this stretch is the superb flight of four locks leading down to Hurleston Junction. Cross over the bridge and turn left onto the Shropshire Union Canal. The canal at this point also follows the Weaver Way. This part of the canal as you approach Barbridge is often very busy and has been called the 'Clapham Junction' of the inland waterways. You may like to cross the bridge (no. 100) to visit the Barbridge Inn for refreshments. Next you cross over the Middlewich Branch of the canal at Barbridge Junction.

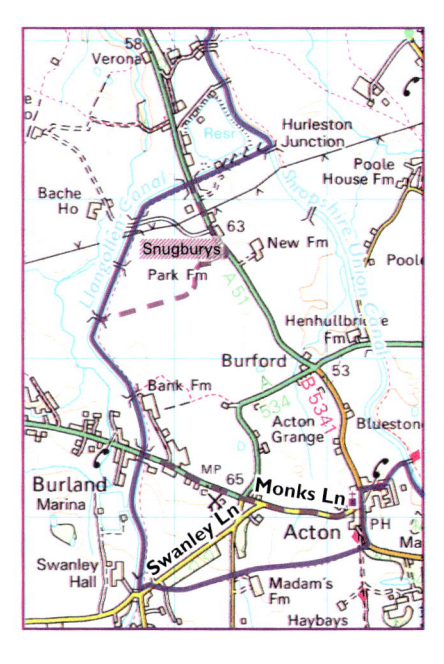

139

SECTION 1 Nantwich to Chester 22.5 miles

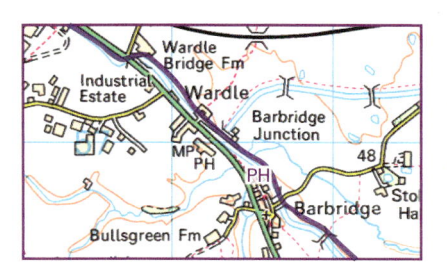

Continue on along the canal, with the A51 on your right and passing Wardle Industrial Estate on your left. Next you pass by Calveley which was once quite a busy place with a number of cheese warehouses. You can find the evidence that there was once a railway station here and it was an important place for transferring goods between canal boats and trains up until 1960. At bridge no. 104 the towpath crosses to the other side of the canal. After a further mile, you reach the locks at Bunbury Wharf. The two locks here are built as a staircase descending 15 feet 7 inches, and are the first ones on the Chester Canal since Nantwich. The magnificent block of stables above the top lock used to have 22 stalls where the fast or 'fly' boats changed horses to enable them to keep up their high speed carriage of important and perishable cargoes. Turn left off the canal here on the road which leads to Bunbury. Take care here as there is no pavement.

After two thirds of a mile you cross a stream and then pass an old mill on your left. The present mill dates from 1840; remarkably, it is still in full operation producing fine flour, as a heritage museum with a pleasant

Disused lime kilns near Bunbury © Candice Smith

STAGE 3 Barbridge to Beeston 4.7 miles

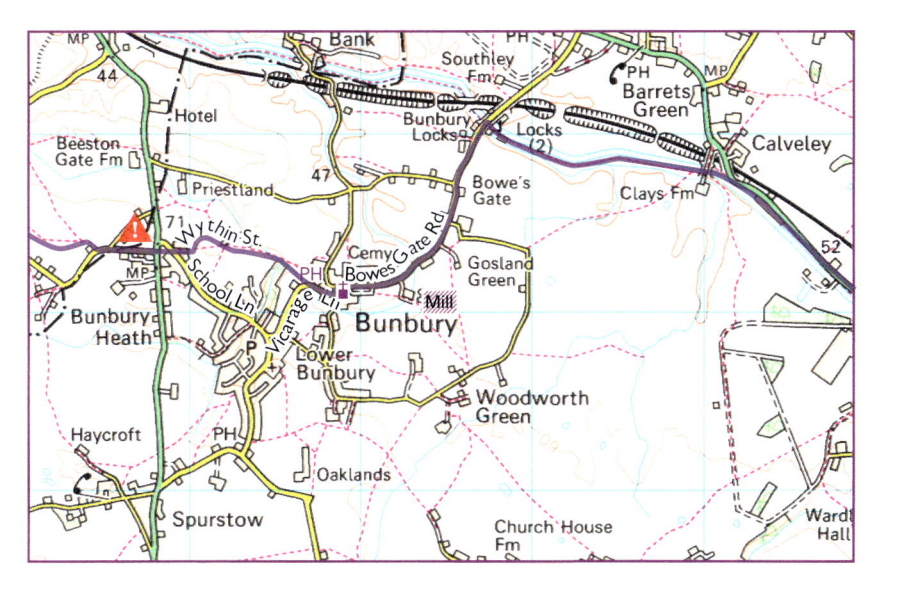

visitor centre. Continue up to the village to the prominent church of St Boniface. For more information about Bunbury and the church, turn to page 38.

From the church, go straight ahead down the hill (Vicarage Lane) and before it bends left, take the path on the right along a farm track. Bear left and cross a bridge over a small stream. Keep to the right hand edge of the field and go through a kissing gate into a strip of woodland. Cross over into the next field by a clump of pine trees and you will find the kissing gate on the other side leading between houses out onto a road which you cross over and turn right to reach the A49.

Bunbury Church Interior © Candice Smith

|41

SECTION 1 Nantwich to Chester 22.5 miles

Cross with care and go on along the road which leads to Beeston. As the road bends to the left, there is a footpath on the right which The Two Saints Way has formerly used, but as this is in dispute at the time of going to press, continue straight on along Moss Lane. Pass roads to Tiverton on your right and Peckforton on your left and then turn right by an attractive timber-framed house up to the castle. For a brief history of Beeston Castle see page 36.

Assuming that you have stopped to visit the castle, turn left to continue on your way, passing Castlegate Farm on your right. As the road starts to circle the castle, the footpath you need is on your right. It leads downhill and passes under the railway and across a bridge to reach the canal at Wharton's Lock where you turn left. At the next bridge you come to the Shady Oak pub where camping is available. After this point, look out for barn owls which can sometimes be seen on the left-hand side where owl boxes have been installed by the Broxton Barn Owl Group. After you have passed bridge no. 111, the canal sweeps round to the left, where you cross an aqueduct over the River Gowy. You may like to slip down the steep path to take a look at the pedestrian tunnel under the canal. After another four miles you will approach Waverton, with the spire of St Peter's prominent on the left.

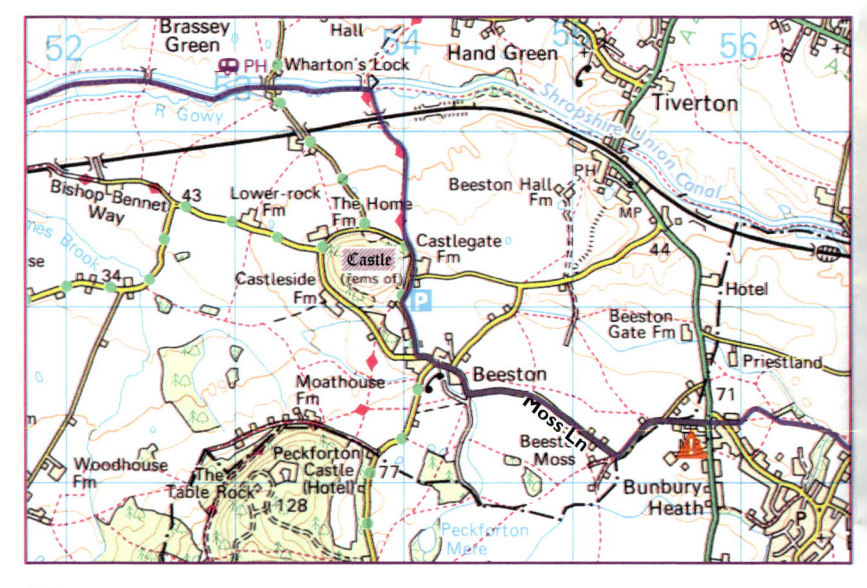

STAGE 2 Beeston to Waverton 8 miles

Beeston Castle © English Heritage

143

SECTION 1 Nantwich to Chester 22.5 miles

As you walk the next mile, you pass Rowton Moor on your left which was the site of one of the last battles in the Civil War. It took place on 24th September 1645 and was decisively won by the Parliamentarians with 600 Royalists killed and 800 taken prisoner. Charles I is said to have watched the battle as it reached the suburbs of Chester from the Phoenix Tower (now known as King Charles Tower) before fleeing to Denbigh.

At the next bridge (no. 120, called Rowton Bridge), you make a final excursion off the Chester Canal before Chester into Christleton. Cross over the bridge and along Rowton Bridge Road. When you reach a crossroads, go straight on into Village Road, passing Christleton High School on your right. Continue up the road. You will pass the Ring O Bells public house on your left. When you reach the village green, take note of the well and the Victorian Pump House. St James' Christleton is ahead of you. For information about St James see page 34.

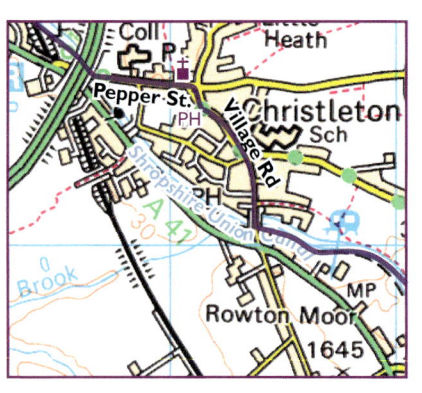

Turn left along Pepper Street. You pass a college on your right and then cross over the canal and descend to the towpath just before it passes under the A55. The canal then crosses over the railway and under the A41 and on into Chester past three locks. The first is Tarvin Road, with a characteristic lock cottage, then comes the curiously named Chemistry Lock, called because a factory here in the 19th century produced naptha. Finally, after the Water Tower you come to Hoole Lane Lock. On the opposite side is a small chapel with an attractive little spire, now converted into houses. This chapel was called St Paul's Mission and was no doubt used as an outreach to boatmen and their families. You finally leave the canal when you reach Russell Street on your left.

At the end of Russell Street, cross over the main road (Boughton) at the lights and continue into Dee Lane. Enter Grosvenor Park on your right and passing a pond on your left, make for the white statue on the central avenue. This is the Second Marquis of Westminster who gave the park to the city in 1867. Turn right here along the avenue of high shapely holly bushes and walk towards St John's Church ahead of you. Walk round to the right of the church to the main entrance on the west side. From St John's Church, cross over the ramp at the Roman amphitheatre. Turn right at this point to cross over the road at the lights and then left to enter through the old city walls through the rounded arch of Newgate.

STAGE 2 Beeston to Waverton 8 miles

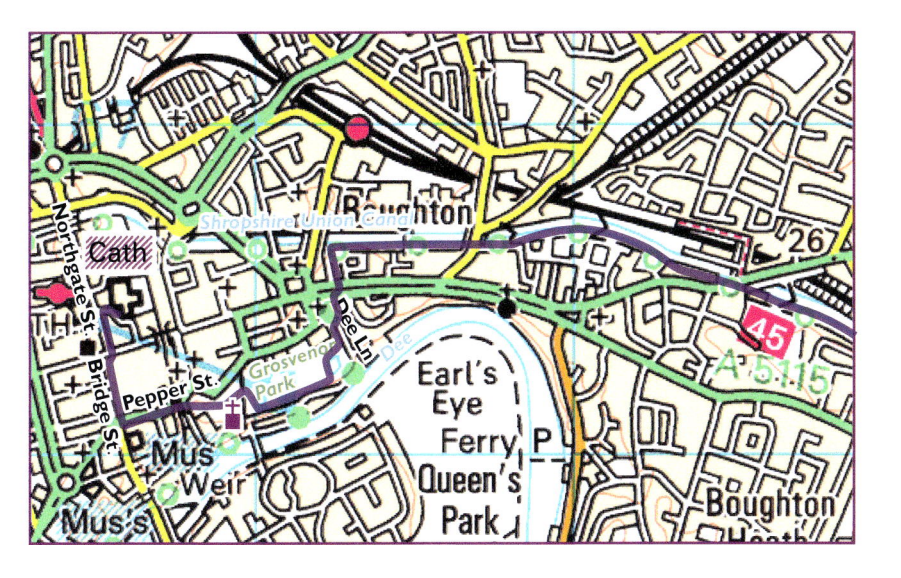

This was formerly called the Wolf Gate or Wulfad's Gate – a reminder to medieval pilgrims of the shrine they may have visited in Stone. Continue under a covered way along Pepper Street before turning right up Bridge Street. Half way up on the right hand side at no. 39 is Spudulike. This is well worth a visit to experience the incongruity of a fast food restaurant juxtaposed with the perfectly preserved section of the Roman baths and hypocaust system in the basement. At the top of Bridge Street, turn right at the Cross and immediately left into Northgate Street. After another 200 yards, opposite the Gothic-style town hall turn right into St Werburgh Street to enter the cathedral. **Be sure you visit the shrine of St Werburgh which is your final destination.**

The Cross © Julie Mitchell

145

Acknowledgements

I would like to thank the following people for their help in the production of this guidebook:

Gordon Emery for his contributions about Chester and the Chester Canal and for proof reading the first part of the publication; Eric and Margaret Harding who provided much helpful information about public transport and accommodation; David Haden for the points of information in North Staffordshire; Stephen Spackman, the site Ranger for the Apedale Community Country Park, for information about the park; John Sparshatt of the Long Distance Walkers Association for providing accurate information on distances; Amanda Kay of Copsewood Editorial Services Ltd for copy-editing the manuscript; Malcolm Down for valuable advice on publishing; Richard Merritt and his team at Spark Design & Communication who have worked tirelessly on the design of this guide and been so consistently helpful. I am grateful to several people who have walked the route and made helpful suggestions for the route description. Finally I wish to thank Marg Hardcastle, Robert Mountford, Tim Saxton and Philip Swan for their consistent support and encouragement

Extracts are taken from *Christleton St James' Church* by David Cummings, published by the author for St James' Church (2007).

Information on religious houses is from *Monastic Staffordshire* by John L. Tomlinson published by Churnet Valley Books (2000).

Cover photo by Paul Graetz.

© David Pott 2015